DEEP IN THE WAVE

DEEP IN THE WAVE

A SURFING GUIDE TO THE SOUL

BEAR WOZNICK

with Lou Aronica

CENTER STREET

New York   Boston   Nashville

Unless otherwise noted, all scripture quotations noted NIV are from The Holy Bible, New International Version® NIV®. Copyright © 1973, 1978, 1984, 2011 by Biblica, Inc.™. Used by permission. All rights reserved worldwide.

Center Street
Hachette Book Group
237 Park Avenue
New York, NY 10017

www.centerstreet.com

Printed in the United States of America

RRD-C

First Edition: July 2012
10 9 8 7 6 5 4 3 2 1

Center Street is a division of Hachette Book Group, Inc.
The Center Street name and logo are trademarks of Hachette Book Group, Inc.

The Hachette Speakers Bureau provides a wide range of authors for speaking events. To find out more, go to www.hachettespeakersbureau.com or call (866) 376-6591.

The publisher is not responsible for websites (or their content) that are not owned by the publisher.

Library of Congress Cataloging-in-Publication Data

Woznick, Bear.
    Deep in the wave : a surfing guide to the soul / Bear Woznick with Lou Aronica.—1st ed.
        p. cm.
    Summary: "World-class surfer Bear Woznick brings us a powerful and entertaining spiritual primer that uses surfing as a metaphor for moving toward God"—Provided by the publisher.
    ISBN 978-0-89296-829-9
    1. Spirituality. 2. Surfing—Religious aspects. 3. Surfers—Religious life. I. Aronica, Lou. II. Title.
    BL624.W685 2012
    204'.4—dc23

                                                                    2012013389

*To my four children, Fawn, Jeremiah, Shane, and Josh,
as well as for those two who await my first kiss in heaven.*

To my parents, Greg and Mereece Woznick.

To my beautiful bride, Talin Heurlin Woznick.

Acknowledgments

I want to thank songwriter and author Melody Green. I took her out surfing many years ago and as we paddled back in, she told me that I had to write a book about what I had been sharing with her in the water. Mahalo to my author friend Anthony Destefano, who first scanned the pages of my manuscript and who greatly encouraged me. I want to thank my literary manager, Peter Miller; and my personal editor, mentor, and Obi-Wan Kenobi, Lou Aronica. He never gave up on me. I want to thank Kate Hartson at Center Street, who believed in me and this book.

I want to thank my parents, Greg and Mereece Woznick, who themselves penned beautiful, inspirational words. My mom laughed through my reading of the first chapter of the very serious western I had tried to write thirty years ago; she thought I was trying to be funny. Well now we can both laugh, Mom. I love you both.

Mahalo to the community at the Benedictine Monastery,

some of whom I have had a relationship with for more than thirty-five years. They provided a quiet place for me to pray and to seek the Lord's leading as this venture began, and they provided prayer cover for me all along the journey. While on private retreat at the Benedictine Monastery, I sensed the Holy Spirit breathe into my heart, "Follow the ancient path." This book is not based on the latest pop culture or pop theology. It is based on the writings of the ancient mystics of the Old and New Testaments as well as St. John of the Cross, St. Therese of Lisieux, St. Teresa of Avila, St. Bernard de Clairveux, and John Paul II. My book follows the pattern of the stages of intimacy with God that they have shared with us. I hope I was faithful in sharing their ancient way and hope to be faithful to them as I continue my soul surfari.

I want to thank the people of Hawaii, especially of the island of Molokai, and the Waikiki beach boys who showed me the way of Aloha. I want to give a shout-out to Marlene, Janice, and Miki at the Pacific Beach Aloha Center Café for the gallons of caffeinated inspiration they provided me on those early mornings. Mahalo to Brian and the crew at the back deck of the Moana, who encouraged me as I wrote under the same Banyan tree that Hemingway, Robert Louis Stevenson, and Jack London enjoyed. Mahalo to John and the crew at the Kale Hoa Oasis, which I call Shangri-la because there in the late afternoons I had my Arthuro Fuente cigars only feet from the beach and wrote into the sunset. I have to thank our many visitors to the islands whose buzz of joyful voices in the background as I wrote lifted me, energized me, and carried me along like so many waves.

Mahalo to Chuck Inman, my personal fitness trainer, who processed with me a lot of the thoughts in these pages between bench presses, and my son Shane Woznick, who joined me every morning at six a.m. for coffee, and whose filmmaking has helped to further this overall project.

I want to thank my beautiful Swedish bride, Talin Heurlin Woznick. We traveled the world for months after we were first married while waiting for her marriage visa approval. This book began just as we began our marriage as we journeyed through Thailand, Sweden, Germany, Estonia, Spain, France, and Italy, and finally to the shores of Waikiki. Writing this book was literally a journey and all along Talin was my constant companion and encourager. Better yet, from time to time, she would draw me away from my efforts to go for a tandem surf.

Mahalo to soul surfers everywhere, whether you ride ocean waves or not.

Mahalo to the Holy Spirit, for He sent me the waves of His Spirit that I felt carry me every step of the way as I sought to flow with Him. "Faithful is He who calls you. For He will do it."

Aloha Ke Akua Ho'omaika'i.
May the breath of God be with you.
Bear Craig William Woznick

Contents

Contents

DEEP IN
THE WAVE

CHAPTER I

Hundred-Year Swell

WINTER 2008

"Dad!"

My oldest of three sons was on the phone. His excitement flooded me like a big wave. "Yeah, Jeremiah?"

"The surf's up! It's big! The biggest surf I have ever seen! Too big to paddle into. Crazy Todd is taking me out so he can tow me in with his Jet Ski."

"You're ready for it. Where are you?"

"Haleiwa Harbor."

"This is what you were made for, son. Go for it."

"Aloha, Dad. I love you."

"I love you, Jeremiah. Aloha."

I knew Jeremiah was in God's hands. I kept my responses to him brief for a reason. If we talked longer, he would sense my tension. At times like this, not saying anything is the best way to stay in a place of faith and grace. My son didn't need to know how nervous I was before he challenged waves of this magnitude.

One of my favorite lines from my favorite film *Big Wednesday* is, "The truth is that in big surf you are always alone. You cannot rely on anyone but yourself." I have experienced this stark truth many times. The waves and currents can separate you from everyone and everything. It's a solitary time when you can rely only on your physical, mental, and emotional strength—and your faith in God.

The last word we said to each other was *aloha*. To Hawaiians, that word is full of meaning. *Ha* means "breath," and *aloha* literally means "to give breath." In big surf, breath can become a precious commodity. Some big wave surfers even carry ten-minute oxygen tanks in case of a long hold-down underwater. Though Jeremiah would desperately need a tank this day, he did not have one.

Aloha also means "love," "hello," and "good-bye." I swallowed hard, as I thought about this, hoping this was not the last time I'd hear my son say, "Aloha, Dad. I love you." I wanted to tell him to be careful, but I bit my tongue, knowing that he didn't need to deal with my being overly concerned for his safety.

Todd Robertson, one of my best friends and one of the best watermen I have ever known, would be towing Jeremiah in. Several years ago, Todd and I decided to be each other's heroes. It's just so much more convenient that way. We bow to each other on the beach saying, "I am not worthy," and run to carry the other's surfboard up from the sand in true acts of hero worship. For good reason, I gave him his nickname "Crazy Todd." Still, I knew Jeremiah was in good hands. In the presence of waves that might on this day exceed seventy feet, I prayed that God's hands would be there too.

Jeremiah was about to experience the awesome power of God in a way very few ever have. When conditions are like this, you can see liquid mountains moving toward shore from miles away. The Hawaiians call these *hehe nalu*, or "mountain waves." These would dwarf the size of the waves in the recent tsunami that hit Japan. Fewer people have surfed waves this size than have climbed Mount Everest. If "the fear of the Lord is the beginning of wisdom" (Psalm 111:10 NIV), then this would be Jeremiah's beginning.

Sometimes, five to ten minutes pass from the time you first see waves this size rising out in the sea until they finally roll in. The waves sweep in from storms more than a thousand miles away. They travel over open ocean and then suddenly hit the shallow coral reefs of Hawaii where there is no continental shelf to slow them down or dissipate their energy. They come out of water more than two miles deep. As they get close to shore, they begin to feel the shallow reef, and they rise up higher and higher until they blot out the sun and throw their shadow over you.

The swell may roll in a set of twenty or more waves. These waves are like the baddest biker gang in town. They just come in, take over, and do whatever they want. About once a year here, a naive visitor to our islands will be standing with his back to the sea while someone else is taking his picture. Then the wave comes and just steals the unsuspecting person away. The very first lesson my dad taught me about respecting the surf was, "Never turn your back on the ocean, son."

I pondered big waves I had ridden as I drove up to the north shore to witness what my son was about to attempt. I basted in my own adrenaline for the forty-five-minute drive, at last turning into Haleiwa Harbor to wait for his return. As I looked out onto the ocean, my heart sank. I had never seen waves this huge. I drove to the end of the harbor, where my youngest son, Joshua, was looking out to the ominous sea.

These waves rolled in at a speed of thirty-five miles an hour—the same speed that a tsunami slows down to when it hits a coastline. That is much too fast to catch lying on a big surfboard and paddling hard. Only the most powerful Jet Skis have the speed to pull surfers into these waves.

The challenge with Jet Skis is that they sometimes get you into the kind of trouble that only Jet Skis can get you out of. If the Ski malfunctions or wipes out and is lost in a big wave, things can get serious very quickly.

"Where is he?" I said when I came up to Joshua.

"I don't know, dude—I mean, Dad." He pointed out to sea. "They are way out there somewhere. I hope they're okay. I lost sight of them right away."

The surf was holding the harbor indicator buoy underwater for more than a minute at a time. Indicator buoys are never supposed to submerge. Joshua and I stood vigil as the sun set, and I thought of stories of surfers who had to swim through the night against mighty currents hoping to stay close enough to shore to find a way in with the sunrise. Some were never found.

An eternity went by and now the sun had just set. Finally, I saw a lone Jet Ski with a lone rider way out past the harbor buoy, which was itself at least a half mile away. The Ski cruised back and forth, waiting for a lull in the breaking waves to make a run to the harbor. If that lull didn't come, the Ski would have to go at least thirty miles to the other side of the island to get in. I hoped this wasn't Crazy Todd, because I could not see my son.

Finally, an opportunity came and the Jet Ski sped into the harbor. My heart sank. It was Todd. Then suddenly, to my great surprise and relief, I saw him. Jeremiah rose from behind Crazy Todd, looking more alive than I had ever seen him. He radiated the clean look of someone who had just gone skydiving or to confession.

Crazy Todd pulled his Ski up to the dock as it sputtered and died. He'd run out of fuel. That was cutting it close.

"How was it?" I said when we approached Jeremiah.

His voice seemed to come from another world. All he said was, "It was big, Dad. It was big."

He didn't seem capable of saying much more at that point, so I didn't press further. Three months later, Jeremiah was finally able to tell me the entire story of the day, the swell, and the waves that made him part of the "big wave tribe."

The first wave that rolled through was around thirty feet. Most surfers have never seen a wave half this size, and far fewer have ever tried to surf one. Todd pulled Jeremiah on the tow-in surfboard, and they made a run along the back of the wave just scoping things out without Jeremiah dropping in. Then Todd towed Jeremiah back out, and Jeremiah let himself sink into the water and relax, breathing deep to saturate his body with oxygen.

Jeremiah had years of experience in all kinds of surf. He had been surfing for as long as he could walk, and he surfed nearly every day. He was in his late twenties and in his prime, as conditioned and prepared as he could be. If anyone was going to handle what he was attempting, it would have to be someone as conditioned on and under the water as he was. We had spent quite of bit of time together in the months leading up to this, building our lung capacity by diving twenty feet down under the ocean, grabbing a big rock, and picking it up and running while holding our breath.

A monster set came out of the northwest. Crazy Todd signaled Jeremiah, and Jeremiah felt the tug of the towrope. His back foot was securely strapped into the tow-in surf-board, but as he whipped into the wave, he could not get his other foot into the front strap. He was essentially surfing with one foot.

When you tow into a wave, the Jet Ski whips you into the wave so that you gain maximum velocity. Then you cut a horizontal path along the wave face. If you go straight down on a monster wave like this, your bottom turn will be too late and the peak of the wave will fall on you, giving you a good minute or two of misery. The wave will crush you and hold you under for the next two or three waves, shaking you like a rag doll in a dog's jaws as sixty feet of water rolls over you. Think about how heavy a bucket of water is, and then think of how it would feel to have fifty Olympic-size pools dumped on you. The only thing you can do in this situation is to try to get into a fetal position so your limbs don't get ripped from your body. Then you hold your breath, try to relax to conserve precious oxygen, and wait for the wave to release you. You are being tossed around so much that you have no sense of up and down. When the wave finally lets you go, you swim away from the dark toward the light. When you surface, you hope you get to gulp in a quick breath before the next wave pounces on you and drills you forty feet deep again.

Jeremiah felt the wave lifting him higher and higher. He looked to the bottom of the wave and calculated that he was six stories high. Finally Todd's Jet Ski pulled him over the lip and whip-turned him. Jeremiah released the towrope and made the drop.

He was immediately in trouble. He was still unable to get his front foot in the strap, and he was dropping straight down into the pit. This was the exact opposite of what he wanted to do. He intended to go down the line horizontally along the wave face toward the safety of the channel over a mile away, but it was too late. He was locked in to this monster wave, surfing with only his back foot secured in the foothold. Luckily, the wave shouldered for a few moments. After he dropped down this sixty-foot face, he was able to bottom turn and shoot back up.

"God must have been smiling on me, because I kicked out the back of it," he told me, grinning a smile back at God as he spoke.

Crazy Todd was smart enough to put Jeremiah on the last wave of the set so another wave wouldn't pummel him. Todd swooped by Jeremiah on the Jet Ski and my son grabbed the towrope and Todd pulled him back out to the safety of deeper water.

As it turned out, though, that was "just the lemon next to the pie." Laughing, Crazy Todd said to my son in Hawaiian pidgin, "You like go deep?" Jeremiah took a long minute to consider this, and finally the yes in him overpowered the fear.

With a look of determination, he quoted one of his surf heroes, Gerry Lopez: "It feels like a good day to die." When a surfer tow-in surfs, he assumes he is going to die but believes in his partner and that he will resuscitate him. If you can't accept that assumption, you should not go.

With that agreement, Todd towed Jeremiah deep into the jaws of nine of the biggest waves ever surfed.

"I felt completely capable and in charge of that moment, yet not in charge at all," Jeremiah recounted. "You know, Dad, whenever I am on the top of a big wave and about to drop in, I always thank God for me making that wave. I thank Him because I feel like I have already ridden it and I know I will make it. God imparted His *manna* to me through that wave. I remember feeling I could do anything after that."

After the tenth wave, Todd rocketed in on his Jet Ski, but he could not get to Jeremiah in time. He could not risk losing the Ski, which would have put both of them in trouble, so he boogied back out to safety. Wave after wave thundered down on top of Jeremiah. Each time, my son went under for half a minute.

Todd made a run for Jeremiah nine times; nine times he was forced back by heavy water. Nine times Jeremiah took a huge wave on the head. Nine times he barely caught a

breath before he was held under long enough to feel his capillaries tingle due to oxygen starvation. Finally, mercifully,
the surge of the waves pushed my son a half mile closer to
shore, and Todd was able to get him. Their only escape,
though, was to go right back out through the incoming surf
to deeper water.

They could not delay to gather their strength or their
thoughts. Todd had to throttle full power over wave after
twenty-foot wave faces to get through the exploding white
water that could cause air to flow into the Jet Ski and cause
it to cavitate and lose power. They flew on. They would land
hard, clear their heads, and look out on another wave, each
time getting increasingly exhausted. On about the twentieth wave, they landed so hard that Jeremiah flew forward.
Without thinking about it, he grabbed for Todd and they
both went off the front of the Jet Ski.

The Ski was rigged with a kill switch tied with a lanyard
to Todd's wrist, so when Todd flew off, the engine stopped.
Todd swam over as quickly as he could and jumped on the
Ski with Jeremiah close behind. Finally, they turned toward
home and made the run to the harbor.

Jeremiah told me, "I could see the sun backlighting and
piercing a luminous green glow through the face of these
death-bomb waves—maybe twenty of them in a row—
marching in. The line of waves extended miles out to sea
like an advancing army. They were dark. They were every

shade of blue and yellow. They were ugly. They were beautiful. I had the thought that maybe in some small way I had experienced the manna of the ancient Hawaiians who knew the power of these big waves and that maybe somehow I had entered that manna and it had entered me."

Jeremiah went big and he went deep that day, and he found a level of soul satisfaction he didn't know existed before. It transformed him forever.

I have been surfing my whole life. It is a source of power for me. For me, not surfing would be like not breathing. I have understood at many levels that there is a connection between the majesty of surfing and the unparalleled majesty of the Almighty, the Big Kahuna. When I watched my son emerge from the water after his experience of going deep, I realized that it was time for me to share the lessons I have learned in the surf, both about surfing and about my spirit. Jeremiah dropping in on those big waves that day inspired me to paddle in and write this book.

A young man once told me, "I am just not a very spiritual person." I responded, "Being spiritual is not an optional extra. You don't have a choice. You are living in a spiritual world. The greatest quest a man can undertake is the challenging journey toward intimacy with God." The message of this book is that it is essential that you accept the challenge and go deep in the wave with God. Just as my son took the biggest challenge of his life to surf monolithic waves, if your life is to have true meaning and fulfillment you need to take the challenge of surfing the deepest swells of the Spirit, for nothing else will satisfy your soul.

Just as a surfer literally abandons himself to a big wave, so we need to learn to go deep and abandon ourselves to the wave of our Creator. When you look out to sea, you can view the beauty and the power of the wave, but you are removed from it. When you paddle into a wave, the experience becomes immediate, personal, and intimate. This book invites you to paddle out and seek that immediacy and intimacy with your Creator.

To go deep means to die to self and live for God. Jeremiah had to contemplate whether this was "a good day to die."

To go deep means total commitment. There is no such thing as partial commitment when you are paddling down the face of a big wave. The surfer must totally want that wave and be completely committed to it. This is even truer if we want to open our hearts to know God's heart and to touch His face as a surfer caresses the face of a breaking wave.

To go deep means to champion a cause greater than you can accomplish without God's help. If the deepest part of you yearns for a challenge that requires you to grow in virtue, there can be no greater challenge than the pursuit of God's will. Yes, there is fear in that, but only in fear can we plumb our depths to discover courageous faith. There is no room for cowards in big surf. To go deep means to leave behind timidity and to take up boldness and faith with the full knowledge that putting yourself in the wildness of God's hands is putting yourself in harm's way. You will be tested with great wipeouts, long hold-downs, and, perhaps worst of all, long seasons where there is just no surf to be found.

To go deep means to experience a depth of communion with God that causes you to detach from earthly pursuits and paddle out. To go deep means to fall deeply into the wave of God's unfathomable, primordial love. Look into the deepest black hole in the universe, and God is there. Look at the brightest of galaxies, and He is there. Look to the ends of the universe and beyond, and you will find Him there. Look beyond time and space and He is there.

His waves await you, but they only come so close. God will draw you, but He will stop at the shoreline, inviting you to detach from the comfort of shore and step off to paddle out to Him in a fearful yet trusting spirit of adventure.

You like go deep?

CHAPTER 2

Spring Swell

1965

It was the time of the spring swell, and the almost man in me sensed an awakening in my soul. It was the season when sets of waves no longer angled in from the north but rolled in directly out of the setting sun and straight on shore. The Alaskan ocean current flowed like a river of cold water from the Aleutian Islands down along the coast through the purple-blue kelp beds a mile off the shores of Monterey Bay in Northern California. That day I could sense a change, for there was a slight warming in the sea and in the air, and, as it turns out, within my spirit.

Screeching seagulls circled as the pelicans made their passes along the wave face, sometimes rising up and dive-bombing into the sea for their delicacies. The gulls cheered them on in the hopes they would have leftovers that night.

Three pelicans flew in perfect formation and they seemed to surf the rhythm of the rise and fall of the sea with their feathers just an inch from the wave face. Who could create so beautiful an expression of grace? On land, the pelican was just plain ugly. Yet on the sea, it was beautiful. *Perhaps*, I thought, *just like me*. On the land, I felt awkward and out of sync with my peers and with life. It all seemed so out of balance until I could run to the embrace of the ocean and bodysurf her waves. It was only in the ocean that I felt free, that I felt at ease. It was only in the power of the sea that I felt I had meaning, that I had significance. Perhaps I was chosen last by the older boys to play schoolyard games, but here, the sea unabashedly said, "I choose you. Come and play."

There was never a time that I arrived at the sea and just stopped at the water's edge. That would have been impossible. I could not contain my excitement. The closer I got, the more thrilled I became, and I always ran to her and threw myself into the waiting arms of the ocean. Sometimes the sea was gloomy and moody, sometimes she was nearly still, sometimes she raged, but always, she was there for me. I learned at this young age that I could bring to her my joy or my sadness and that she would accept me. The ocean was my very own come-as-you-are party. She unconditionally accepted me and whatever I brought to her.

It was the age of Moondoggie and Annette Funicello and beach party movies. The Gidget film and TV show propelled thousands of new surfers to flock to the beach and flop on their surfboards like so many floundering fish. These wannabes soon learned just how hard it was to surf. After experiencing their first wipeout, many of them just ended up posing on the sand next to their boards, never venturing to paddle out again. I remember seeing one car where the poser obviously did not surf because he had bolted his surfboard permanently to the rooftop. I was younger, so I was among the last of those who rode the carefree waves of the Gidget era.

The sea grasped my attention and held my heart, as if in suspended animation. Even now my surfboard is like a time machine carrying me back to those days, transforming me into a young surf "grommet," alive and at play.

As a child, before I learned to surf, I would run along the shoreline and play with the waves. I would stand squared to the shore break in a fighter's stance, punching the waves as they broke upon me. I would fight not to yield until one of the waves would finally pick me up like a linebacker and slam me to the sand. I would hold my breath and keep fighting with this imagined adversary as it pummeled me and held me down.

Then once, as the wave picked me up and tumbled me, I just relaxed and let it carry me. I found a certain comfort and then a very real sense of freedom in abandoning myself to the wave. I had no brothers to roughhouse with, so it was the surf that toughened me up. It was the surf that became my father, brother, uncle, and mentor, and in this way the ocean began to impart its *manna* ("power") and *manao* ("wisdom") to me.

It was the time of heavy, single-finned longboards, though I rarely had access to one. Like other boys my age who watched westerns and wanted a horse, I watched surfers and wanted a board. I satisfied my surf cravings by bodysurfing, and I surfed the waves for hours on end. I learned to swim as hard as I could to match the wave's speed in just the right place to find the open face, and bodysurf down the line. To me, bodysurfing was the most intimate I could ever hope to be with creation. Even then, I sensed that being one with the wave was in some way being one with my Creator.

I began to build a knowledge of waves, tides, and currents, and the effects that different ocean bottoms and land structures had on waves. Once I rode my first wave, I looked at all waves differently. I imagined myself surfing every wave I saw, and analyzed each for its fun-in-the-sun potential. I learned that there was a rhythm to the ocean and that waves came in sets. Sometimes, there were three waves to a set; sometimes more than ten. The bigger the surf, the more waves in a set and the longer the time interval between wave peaks. I learned to sense when a swell was building or when it was fading and what direction it was coming from. I learned to discern multiple swells from different distant storms running through the lineup at different angles, sizes, and speeds. I learned how different wind directions could ruin and crumble the waves or sculpt them to perfection.

I thought of myself as invincible, and the surf held no fear for me. I learned that the undertow all moms warned about was essentially a myth, but that strong ocean currents and riptides could sweep me out to sea or down the coast in just a matter of minutes, and I learned how to swim at a right angle to them to escape their grasp. I understood that new moons and full moons affected the tides dramatically, and I learned low tide usually meant longer rides and that it was at low tide the clam diggers arrived with their strange pitchforks and dug for pismo clams. I learned that the power of the wave subsided a bit as the tide went from high to low, and strengthened a bit as it went from low to high, so that the best time to surf longer, more powerful waves was just as the tide started going from low to high.

I learned that some beaches seemed to have perfect surfable waves while others did not, and I wondered why. I would beg my parents to go to the beach, and once they finally agreed, I would begin pleading with them to go to certain beaches where the waves broke best.

The first generation of blown-foam fiberglass surfboards had replaced the hollow wooden surfboards of the previous generation, which in turn had replaced the hundred-plus-pound solid wood boards of an earlier generation of surfers that dated back fifteen hundred years in Hawaii. These were the days before we leashed our boards to our ankles, so wipeouts could result in spectacular sights of surfboards rocketing high in the air, spinning in the breeze, and then coming down like a missile on top of the surfer's head. I witnessed surfers hanging on for dear life to their leashless boards not wanting to lose them. I would see them being sucked up and over the falls, desperately clinging to their boards.

The primary rule of surfing now is that the surfer closest to the peak owns the wave. In the mid-sixties, though, the tribal elders had not yet adopted that concept. So we shared waves, and in so doing shared even more spectacular wipe-outs. More than once I saw two surfers clinging to their crisscrossed boards getting jacked up and tossed together over the lip of a cascading wave. On big days, surfers spent as much time swimming to retrieve their boards as they did paddling them back out. Woe to the unsuspecting citizens playing near shore as heavy boards would explode toward them sideways in the shore break.

When a surfer lost his board, it often seemed to surf better without him on it. The board would continue like a riderless horse, while the surfer floundered in the impact zone. It was as if the ocean and the boards were as alive as the surfers.

There was nothing complex or sophisticated about the

board designs then. The thought of twin fins, tri-fin thrusters, and strange board shapes had not yet entered the minds of the board shapers. Fins themselves had been added to boards only thirty years earlier. These helped surfers stabilize and turn their boards. The design experiments were limited to how much curve or rocker there would be in the nose and tail, whether the nose and tail were rounded or came to a point, and how hard or soft the curve of the rails of the board would be. It was the time of simplicity of thought and design. It was the time of One God, One Country, One Fin.

Sitting on our surfboards in the lineup caused our inner thighs to rub raw against the rails of our boards, so we learned to cut off our ragged Levi blue jeans so they ran halfway down our thighs protecting them from the rail. No one ever thought of wearing store-bought shorts. While others on the beach wore their tight short "bathing suits," surfers started wearing their own invention: "baggies." A cottage industry sprang up in surf towns. Surfers' girlfriends and moms got caught up in sewing long loose-fitting surf trunks. This was the birth of the surfing industry. In time, many surfers came to disdain it more than the growing "military-industrial complex." I went to school with the O'Neill girls, whose father and uncle created the first surf wetsuits. We all became expert artists in math class doodling the O'Neill logo on our notepads.

The water was so cold that, for most of the year, duck-diving through an oncoming lip of a wave meant an ice-cream headache before coming out the other side. The top part of the wetsuit was made with a ducktail that passed between our legs and snapped on the other side to keep it snug. The bottom of the wetsuit came up high above the waist. During the warmer days of the spring swell, some surfers only surfed with the wetsuit top, and the ducktail would flap in the wind as he surfed down the line.

Most young surf grommets did not own a surfboard much less a wetsuit, and many surfers balked at the lack of soul in wetsuit technology; as they put on the constricting wetsuit, they also felt a constriction to their sense of freedom in the water. The solution to the freezing cold water was obvious: don't get wet. So surfers kicked out of a wave early so they would not have to paddle out through white water, and instead of lying down to paddle, they knelt down, leaned over, and knee-paddled. It was not just a style then; it was a necessity.

Long hours of knee-paddling resulted in a phenomenon that no longer exists among surfers today: surfer knots or surfer bumps. Surfers would develop knots on their knees and on the tops of their toes from paddling in that position. To have a surfer knot meant you were a true surfer, not just a poser. It was a mark of distinction. It was a mark of being cool when being cool was everything.

My parents did not know what surfer knots were, nor did they know that I would sneak to the beach and surf, but my mother became concerned when she saw a strange "growth" on my right foot, wondering if she should take me to a doctor. The knot is still on my foot. The only way to get rid of it would be to stop surfing.

These were the days before we could phone for the recorded surf report, and it was way before the Internet. The weatherman only spoke of local conditions, never of low-pressure systems a thousand miles out to sea that might create a wind fetch to drive waves toward the beach two days later. So we looked to the surf gurus—the old men of the sea (anyone over thirty)—for their sage thoughts about the swell. They could sense a growing swell, or so it seemed. "Steamers will be going off tomorrow, six- to ten-foot faces." They missed it more than they got it right, but when they got it right, we credited them with godlike status. As surfers rode back from the beach in their woodies and VW buses, they would stick their hands out to signal to surfers driving down to the beach what the conditions were. We would flash a thumbs-up or a thumbs-down, or rock our palms in a "so-so" motion. Before the age of cell phones there was a coconut telegraph, and surfers had a way of getting the word out to each other. But invariably the news of good waves traveled slower than snail mail. The first words you often heard as you arrived at the beach were the words the film

Endless Summer made famous: "You really missed it. You should have been here yesterday."

It was the coming of age of the surf culture, and it was the coming of age for a generation of surfers. We were rebels without a clue with few tribal elders to lead the way. We did not know that we were setting a trend and birthing a new kind of cool. We just wanted to surf. We all knew we were into something new, something powerful, and most of us perceived beyond that there was a spiritual cool that came with being one with a wave. Just like surfers are drawn to drop deeper and deeper into the wave and ride deeper and deeper inside the tube, so many of us were drawn deeper into the spiritual cool. We became the soul surfers, and to this day it warms the aloha in my weather-beaten, storm-tossed soul to know that I can still count myself among them.

My first memory of surfing was when my parents came home after a long trip and sat on my bed in Velva, North Dakota. They told me the great news that my dad had accepted a position and the family was returning to California to the town of Aptos near Santa Cruz. When we arrived at our new home, my parents, my three sisters, and I drove along the cliffs overlooking Stearns Wharf and along a surf spot that surfers had named Steamers Lane because of the big ships that would pass near that point of land. Hundreds of people stood lining the edge of the cliff, looking down and watching the surfers dodge seals, rocks, leathery kelp, and each other. Some surfers stood along the cliff face, leaning their longboards against themselves like the long lances the Indians held as they looked down from the cliffs at the wagon train they were about to attack in the westerns that all boys my age loved to watch.

I was almost ten years old when we moved there, and I had never seen waves before. From that day, I was never the same. From that day, I was betrothed to the ocean. Year after year, my love for her and understanding of her deepened. Her siren song has never stopped calling me.

We spent all day at the beach. The spring swell kept her promise of offering slightly warmer water, and the sun had done its job and burned off the morning coastal fog. I body-surfed all day long. My mother, as she always did, made me take time-outs under a towel until my cold, purple lips "at least turned a little blue."

The sun began setting, which invited the gentle breeze to turn toward shore. This chilled me, so I sat farther back from the seashore, sheltered among the big rocks along the base of Seacliff Beach. I buried my feet in the silty sand, hoping to warm them just a bit as I watched the rising tides wash away yet another one of my sandcastles. A passing sailboat caught my eye. I watched her sail farther and farther out to sea, and I considered that she needed no fuel, only the wind to fill her sails. The only limit to her journey was the limitations of her captain's vision. I knew that she could go anywhere in the world, and with that realization, a stirring grew in me, a longing for what lay beyond the horizon, not only of the sea but of my soul. I sensed something expanding within me.

My eyes finally lost sight of the sail as it crossed over the horizon and so my gaze drifted back toward the swells that flowed through the kelp beds and then broke in perfect, long lines of surf. One surfer sat on his surfboard like a lone sentry, rising and falling with the swells, looking out to sea, searching for that perfect wave.

Just then, it was as if the universe had opened before me. I realized that these waves had been breaking here long before I was born. The decaying cement ship at the end of the pier reminded me that my time here on earth would end soon enough too and then I would be just be like one of my sand castles: here and then gone. Instead of growing sad, I grew curious, and then I contemplated the nature of the Creator of all I beheld.

Wave after timeless wave breaking on the shore drew me into a contemplation of God's eternity. As a young boy I did not understand that God lived in the eternal now, so I thought of God in a linear dimension of time and space; the one who always was and always will be. I thought of each wave as being a pulse from the very heartbeat of God.

The powerful surf awakened me to the reality that the Creator was all powerful. The beauty of the sea called to me of God's own beauty, and the depth of the sea called to me of the depth of the Creator's love.

All of this was in an instant. As I sat on the edge of the sea, the threshold of all that was and will ever be opened before me. My heart journeyed beyond the horizon and quested deeply within me to know the mysteries of my Creator. There was a "knowing" in me and yet, even more, a not knowing, for the knowing wanted more.

A boy sat down that day upon that rock of contemplation; a young man stood up and walked away. Thus began my venturing. I did not know then that my journey would take me to hell and back. Just then, all was promise. It was the time of awakening. It was the time of the spring swell.

CHAPTER 3

The Summer Swells

1966–1971

It was the time of hippies, flower power, and love-ins. It was called the "Summer of Love," but it was the warm summer swells that captured me. I craved the wave. In my early teens, I fell in love with the ocean. This wasn't a summer fling or even the adoption of a passion. It was something much, much deeper. The ocean was everything to me. I was Romeo, and the ocean was my Juliet. And like that forbidden romance, forces did their best to keep us apart.

My parents, convinced that surfers were rebels on the fringes of society, sought to keep me from joining their tribe. Surfing was completely foreign to them. They grew up in the landlocked Midwest, so how could they know? What they didn't understand was that nothing could have pried me from my beloved. Surfing was deep within my soul.

I would pedal my bright blue Schwinn Sting-Ray, with its saddle seat and mini ape-hanger handlebars, over the eight miles of hills from my home down to the shore. Since my parents disapproved of my surfing, I did not have a surfboard. This hardly mattered, though. If I could not borrow one at the beach, I would just bodysurf. Bodysurfing is a great way for a beginning surfer to get to know the feeling and flow of the surf because you are deep in the wave, not on it. You feel the tug of the receding wave pulling you out toward the next wave that is already rising up. You feel the crosscurrents pulling you sideways to the beach. You feel the unevenness of the ocean bottom as it goes from sandy to rocky shallows and then deepens.

Every real surfer wants to be one with the wave, not just to ride the wave. My body—and my soul—was becoming the wave itself. I was one with the wave. My exhilaration came in letting go and releasing myself to the flow and power of the wave.

I would bodysurf until it drained me of every ounce of energy. Then I would change inside my towel, taking off my cutoff blue jeans and putting on a pair of warm corduroys and the buffed suede shoes we called floaters. If I was not too intimidated by the blank stares of the Vietnam vet hippie surfers wearing their green army jackets with flowers embroidered on them, I would ease my way close to one of their campfires and listen as they played their guitars and smoked their weed.

I was just a young surf grommet and I looked up to these surfers, even though I was invisible to them. I would warm myself and hold my wet cutoffs in front of me, close to the fire, to dry them. When I saw the afternoon fog begin to roll in from the sea, I would tie my cutoffs to my handlebars and pedal my bicycle along the back roads over the hills, racing the fog as it cascaded up and over the sea cliffs and then up the hills from the small town of Aptos to the smaller inland village of Corralitos. As I rode, a sensation would invariably come over me. Something would replace the sense of exhausted satisfaction I had been feeling on the beach; it was a sense of longing, a sense of separation from the one I wanted to be with the most. It was the ache that cannot be relieved, which I would someday equate with both spiritual and romantic longing. For now, though, I longed for the ocean—and for what the ocean brought out in me. There was a deeper draw, as if the Creator of the waves was calling me to Himself.

My parents continued to stand between me and the ocean, but their worries were unfounded. The surfing tribe was distinctive from every other tribe out there, but we were not rebels. While everyone else was getting into trouble at late-night parties, the real surfers would cash it in early so we could dawn patrol the glassy morning surf. A rebel pushes against the system. Surfers don't really do that; instead we just turn our back on the system as if it were not even there. We prefer gazing out to the horizon, waiting for the perfect wave. Given everything that was going on in the world, and particularly in California at that time, my parents should have been far more concerned about my losing interest in surfing and joining another tribe.

For surfers, nothing else holds any value compared to the waves. Our quest is solely to ride those perfect waves. We give up possessions, careers, and relationships to devote ourselves to surfing. Even at this young age I began to learn the lessons of detachment. The ocean drew me to detach from temporal values, meaningless pursuits, and the detours of bad choices that might keep me from my beloved. As soon as I paddled from shore and entered the sea, I knew I was in God's hands.

We have the sense that the perfect wave is rolling out there in the night and will greet us when we paddle out and then wait for it to appear just over the horizon. Every surfer asks the question, "Which would you give up first: sex or surf?" This is a rhetorical question, though. Every real surfer knows that his desire to be one with the wave supersedes any desire for earthly union. For real surfers the waves are as necessary as water is to live and to thrive. Among surfers, there's a saying: "If you used to surf, you never surfed." If someone is capable of giving up surfing, they never truly grasped it; they never really surfed. I had more than one girlfriend say to me, "If you really loved me, you would move inland." My only possible response is, "Would you want me to die? How can I live without water to sustain me?" I wonder where those women are now. I'm guessing at least a few of them are discontentedly landlocked and feeling somehow that they have lost their sense of wonder.

Surfers are unique. Unlike athletes who perform in team sports, surfers are solitary. Even when we paddle out with our friends we are there alone. There is very little conversation in the water (unless Crazy Todd is there) and each surfer finds his own spot in the lineup and waits for his wave. We ride custom surfboards personally shaped for just the type of waves we ride and our own unique way of riding them.

Though we are part of a tribe, we are essentially alone. Surfing draws us into the serenity of solitude. This has been increasingly true for me. I came to know that in the pursuit of intimacy with God, though I might be part of an organized tribe, I would be making an ongoing series of personal decisions. Each of us must go one-on-one with God. As I grew older, I usually rode my motorcycle alone, pedaled my mountain bike alone, hiked alone, flew alone, and even sailed my Catalina alone. I learned to detach from others and, in finding myself, found a longing for the one who gave me the gift of my very life.

I began to realize that, like surfing, my quest for God would be an individual journey. Though there was a spiritual tribe around me, for I had been raised in a church, my response to God's call had to be a unique and personal one.

Over the years, I'd heard people try to define God by their own standards. That always seemed foolish to me. To me, the God who created the universe and sent the waves was exactly who He was. It was not my place to twist God into the fashion and the way I wanted Him to be. My quest was to discover His nature, who He really is. I knew I could not transform Him into an image that suited me. It was I who needed to be transformed, to be like Him to the fullest extent possible, for in doing only that could I hope to see Him face-to-face.

Surfers don't share the same wave, and though I was part of a spiritual tribe, no one could ride that wave for me. I wanted truth and I wanted real experience rather than secondhand information. I did not just want to know *about* God; I wanted to actually *know* Him.

Surfers learn to step off the beach into the deeper water of the shore break. We detach from the security of the land. The Latin root of the word *holy* means "to be without earth." The minute I push off the land and onto my board I am no longer grounded. Everything that I thought stabilized me is gone.

To be holy means to turn our back on the earth. It means to turn our back on the world as it tugs and pulls. It means to turn our back on even our friends and family, on careers and on possessions, and to paddle out into the deep wave of God's love and wait on Him, to rest in Him and wait for that perfect wave that only He can send.

When I sit on my board, I am not in rebellion. I am not even thinking of what sits behind me. I am lost in reverie hoping for a wave. My heart detaches from earthly values and cares, and quests beyond the reaches of the sea. I remember the first time I went out deeper and deeper into the waves until I could no longer touch the ocean bottom. I had to commit to detach, to swim off into the deep sea and wait for the wave. I pushed off and swam out, and suddenly found myself free from the land. I swam and caught wave after wave. I experienced the rush as I slid along the wave face directing my flow with my arms, and twisting my body to maintain control.

Anyone who has spent much time in the ocean knows the rest of this story. In time, a much bigger wave just seemed to come out of nowhere. I could not get away from it, so I turned and swam farther out as the wave sucked me back. It picked me up, lifted me, and flipped me over. It tossed me and then held me down. I had no control at all over what was happening to me. I was freaking out and disoriented, thinking I was running out of air. Instead of just relaxing and going with the flow, I scrambled desperately. I kicked out to try to get my feet to push off the bottom, but instead felt my nose scraping sand.

Then suddenly, I surfaced and I was free. I came out sputtering and laughing. It was fearful and yet liberating. I had yielded all control to the wave, and it suddenly felt great.

Many who survive this relatively harmless experience never venture out that far again. They will never put themselves in a position of not having control. This is unfortunate, because the freedom to let go liberates us from clinging to a false sense of security. For me, the ultimate lesson here was that I needed to let go and let the wildness of God take over.

When I am training with a partner doing tandem surfing beach lifts—practicing raising her above my head as I will later do in the ocean on a board—onlookers will sometimes think they are doing us a favor by stepping up and supporting the girl. Even though I cannot see that happen I am keenly aware when someone has even just barely touched her. When this happens we can no longer feel the sweet spot of our point of balance. In the same way, the world tries to reach out and make us stay on its center of balance and in so doing tries to rob of us of our own real personal center of balance and our sense of the wave of God in our lives. We need to find our own balance.

Back in the late sixties all of this was only beginning to dawn on me. My parents, ever wary of my attraction to surf culture, mistook this sense of detachment for rebellion and attempted to restrict my connection to the ocean. They tried to keep me from the beach, to keep Romeo from Juliet, but they only succeeded in making me more inventive in my ability to sneak away for a secret rendezvous. Once I got my driver's license, it became even harder for them to hold me away from the water.

One night, however, they dealt me a blow I never saw coming. They came home from a business trip and announced that we were moving to the heart of Texas. The *landlocked* heart of Texas. I was devastated, and they thought I was reacting this way because I was going to be separated from my girlfriend.

But when they broke this news to me, I was only thinking about my first love: the sea.

CHAPTER 4

Search for the Perfect Wave

1971–1973

Everything was different in the heart of Texas. There was plenty of sand around me, but no beach, and no waves. There were bluebonnets, and katydids, and mesquite, and people ate things I'd never heard of, like chicken-fried steak, and drank things I'd never seen, like iced tea.

Instead of gliding along the perfect, glassy, cool waves of Monterey Bay, I spent the summer before my senior year of high school cutting down trees with a chainsaw. While all my friends back in California were waxing up their boards and paddling out, I sweated off pounds of water in 95 percent humidity. It was nearly a hundred degrees in the shade. Except that there was no shade—because I was busy cutting all the shade down.

I was landlocked, almost literally a fish out of water. The

39

centeredness of my being was the Pacific Ocean. My inner compass oriented west to a body of water 1,250 miles away. When I sat in class, when I worked, or when I slept, I always knew which way the Pacific was. Unconsciously, I always sat down facing it.

My new friends would ask me what it was like to leave my school and my girlfriend behind. I missed my girlfriend, but they did not understand that what I missed the most was the sea. On my last night in California, I went down to the ocean alone. I swam out as far as I dared into the cold Pacific surf, and then turned and swam back to the shore. I knelt down by the shoreline and scooped sand and water into small glass bottles. For years, I slept with those sacred chalices beside my bed.

Since I had no choice, I threw myself into the life of a Texan. I never once said, "Boy howdy" or "Y'all come back now," but I was determined to make the best of it. The football team needed a fullback, so I played football. Meanwhile, the students seemed so fascinated with the new blond-haired, blue-eyed surfer boy from California that they voted me vice president of the senior class just four weeks after I started school.

Like everything else, the girls were different there. The hippie beach girls of California were into the natural look then and rarely wore makeup. However, the Southern belles were extremely refined in their makeup and clothing, and they even did their nails. They also had this thing I had only seen in the movies, called "dating." In California, we all just hung out together and at some point you discovered you had a girlfriend. In California, there was no "dinner and a movie." In Texas, though, they started going on chaperoned dates in junior high school and had "coming out" cotillion dances and debutante balls. "Coming out" in California meant something completely different.

There was this horrifying event at the end of the date called "walking the girl to the brightly lit front door." I would rather have taken a huge wipeout on my head than have to do that. I was out of my league, and I hid out as best I could from the Southern belles. At the end of the football season, though, I learned that each football player had two or three girls assigned to him, who had been secretly giving him presents and messages to cheer him on. At the end of the season, the football players would find out who their particular girls were and then we had to take each girl out to dinner.

If they had warned me that I would have to endure this before I signed up for football, I would have probably signed up for bull-riding instead. I decided the only way to handle this was to confess my secret fears to my secret cheerleaders. I told them that I was clueless and horrified about the door thing. "Don't worry," they said. "Take us all out at the same time on a triple date and we will show you the Cowboy Way." They taught me to hold the hand of the girl on the way to the door. At the doorstep, I was to turn to face her while reaching my other hand toward hers. If she took my hand, it was a sign for me to lower my head like a fullback and plant one on her lips.

After high school, I went to Baylor University on the other side of town. I was a Catholic adrift at a Southern Baptist university. Going to Baylor was like going back in time. The entire country was erupting in anti-Vietnam protests, but when the local activists threw a protest rally at Baylor, no one bothered to come. I began to go back to my California roots. My hair grew longer and my beard grew fuller. I identified more with the hippies back home than the local goat-ropers, and realizing this made me feel even more lost and landlocked.

Baylor was one of the last schools in the country where the girls had curfews and where men were not allowed at any time in the women's dorms. This led to a few radical practices that I am sure no longer exist anywhere in the universe. I never hear talk of panty raids now, but back then, the entire freshman and sophomore classes of this conservative bastion would stand beneath the eight-story girls' dorms and call for "silk." Meanwhile, because the girls had to be in at ten thirty on weekdays and one a.m. on the weekends, everyone rendezvoused back at the women's dorms about twenty minutes before curfew. Virtually the entire nine-thousand-member student body was there making out. We called this phenomenon the "mush rush." It was the walking-the-girl-to-the-doorstep thing gone quantum.

At curfew, though, the women cloistered themselves in their dorm. You can imagine how amped up this left the men. Between the men's and women's dorms was a big football field that we could illuminate at night. We wound up playing a lot of late-night football games. We became obsessed with completing "the perfect pass," which we defined as a receiver running full speed on a long post route with a tight spiral arching directly over him into his outstretched hands. The receiver would haul it in at full sprint and then run for the goal line.

We spent months trying to complete such a pass, and one night we accomplished it. It was two a.m. when Bobby Dickerson and I executed this perfect play. He split the defenders and ran as far as he could as I arched a long spiral. He looked up and extended his hands just as the ball floated into them. He caught it in full stride and sprinted across the goal line and through the end zone.

Then he kept on going. He sprinted across the small bridge over Baylor Creek and into the night. We finally realized that he wasn't coming back and that he had run away with our only football, so we gave chase over the bridge and all over campus. We saw him in the distance holding up the football in front of the women's dorms and yelling for silk. When he spotted us coming, he took off again. We eventually caught him by the bear pits, where Baylor had several live bears. He was talking to the biggest and oldest bear, "the judge," and telling him all about the "perfect" pass and catch.

What is this instinct in man to seek perfection? Surfers long for that perfect surf spot on that perfect day and that perfect wave. The search for the perfect wave is the essence of a real surfer, but what I've come to learn is that the search for perfection is a deep instinct in the very core of humanity's being. At Baylor, we were required to take religion classes, and I remember a professor reading a scripture verse one day that woke me up. Jesus said, "Be perfect, therefore, as your heavenly father is perfect" (Matthew 5:48 NIV). *What does that mean?* I wondered. *Could that even be possible?*

It was like something the Dalai Lama would say, or maybe Jonathan Livingston Seagull. Was it a command? Was I somehow supposed to strive to meet perfection? Because if I was, He was asking the wrong guy. But the thought came to me that maybe these words were more an act of creation than a commandment. "Be perfect" sounded like a creation verse like "Let there *be light*." Maybe these words were a creative statement to which I could open myself. This caused my soul to become increasingly restless. I realized that my desire for the perfect wave was all wrapped up inside something else. I realized that this desire for perfection was actually a desire for the Perfect One.

I searched for that perfection in school grades and in Asian martial arts. I even searched for that perfection by taking an advanced philosophy class. Twelve of us sat with the professor around a beautiful wooden table surrounded by the ancient books of the great philosophers. In those books were written philosophies from the Cynics to Plato, from Confucianism to Nietzsche. Certainly, I would find the perfect wave here. Unfortunately, while we dug into different philosophies each week, they all fell short for me. So many seemed almost right, almost true, but every one of them fell short in my estimation. I knew that there was no almost truth; that's the essence of a lie.

Then it was time to study C. S. Lewis. In his atheism, C. S. Lewis had come to a point where he began to ponder the cross and it seemed to him to be the missing piece of the puzzle. He had said that if you lived in a land where it was always cloudy and you could not prove there was a sun, you could still surmise that there was one because it illumined everything. The light of the cross was the only thing that illumined everything for him. To me, this made everything else make sense.

I still believed that there was an ultimate causality, that there was a God, but still God seemed distant and impersonal to me. I thought of Him as a father who sent child support checks by way of the sun and rain to provide for my sustenance, but He was not a personal God who loved me enough to lift me up and look in my eyes. I would drift off to sleep at night next to those bottles of ocean water and sand, remembering the yearning I had felt in my youth when eternity seemed to open out before me. The water had evaporated from the bottles and only the sand remained. This seemed symbolic to me.

I would nod off to sleep remembering the exhilaration of bodysurfing. Bodysurfers spend a great deal of time in the barrel of the waves. We almost have to be in the barrel to catch it and we can easily sideslip and tuck into it. I would imagine that moment when I was riding deep inside a barrel looking out of the opening in front of me. I could still hear the sound of rushing water sometimes as loud as thunder echoing off the inside of the wave as I was locked in. I relived that moment when I was going at the same speed of the wave and all I saw was the light shining from the opening of the barrel in front of me. There was no sense of location and no feeling of movement. There was a surge of energy and motion and yet no movement. It was as if time stood still as I was one with the wave. I longed for that with my Creator.

At that time, with what little understanding I had of God, I was trying my best to live an upright life. But I was doing it on my own power, and I was more up*tight* than up*right*. I focused on the dos and don'ts, seeking more to appease God than please Him. Then, without warning, in the summer before my junior year in college, a tsunami of God's love came into my life.

My mom had been inviting me to go to a "prayer meeting."

To me, this sounded terribly boring, but she kept trying. She said that there was an almost tangible presence of God there. I trusted my mother. I knew her to be careful, wise, and discerning, so I knew she wasn't saying these things lightly.

"Who goes to these prayer meetings?" I asked.

"There is a Catholic priest and some nuns," she said, "a theologian from Baylor, an Assembly of God minister, a rocket scientist, a Notre Dame graduate, and just normal people."

It still sounded boring.

"And a few cute girls," she added.

It was getting more interesting.

"And if you come, I'll buy you a pair of blue jeans."

She'd sold me.

At the meeting, I immediately felt something different, something special. There seemed to be a glow in the room. She introduced me to the rocket scientist Charles Debois, and then Vietnam vet Bob Schwartz introduced himself. He broke out his guitar, and one of the cute girls sat next to him with hers. They handed out copies of songs and we began to sing. The songs were not just about God but were more like prayers to God.

There seemed to be no form to the evening. There was singing and praying, and then someone would share a thought or an experience. Though it all seemed to be freeform, it was far from random. God's spirit seemed to weave everything together in a perfect poem, as if God Himself was speaking to us. Everyone seemed to feel that God was really listening—and that they were listening to God as well. There seemed to be a sense of true intimate communion with God.

There was something tangible at that prayer meeting. Nothing extraordinary happened, but somehow I knew something deep and real was going on. Someone read, "*Perfect* love casts out fear, he that fears is not made *perfect* in love" (see 1 John 4:18). There was that word *perfect* again. I was not afraid. I wanted the experience of intimacy with God that they had. Afterward, I spoke to the guitar player and the rocket scientist, asking how I could experience the intimacy with God they very obviously had.

"It's simple," the rocket scientist said. "God is the one inviting you and so it is He who makes this happen. You just need to surrender all you are to God. We will pray for you to be immersed in His spirit."

I'd learned that when a big wave is in front of you, you don't hesitate. I saw this big, beautiful wave of God's love, and I wanted to paddle into it now.

"I'm in," I said.

The guitarist shook his head. "No. Not now. You really need to think about this first, because this truly is surrendering all that you are to God. This will cost you everything. *Everything*. You will need to lay down every ambition, every ounce of pride, every dream, and surrender it all to Him. If you really want this, read through the Book of Acts and the Gospel of John, pray, and come back next week. If you are really sure then, we will pray for you."

The Monday night before the next prayer meeting, I dreamed that God was walking toward my apartment. I was thrilled to see Him. I opened the door before He could knock and went to hug Him. His eyes were so piercingly full of love, but a deep sense of my own unworthiness came over me. As I reached to hug Him, I found myself falling at His feet and holding His leg. But I had a sense everything was going to be okay.

At the prayer meeting the next night, they asked me if I still wanted to be prayed for, and I said yes. We went into the back bedroom. I did not know that they had fasted all day asking for God to empower me with His Spirit. Soon after we started, Bob casually touched me as he was about to ask something—and out of nowhere the tsunami hit me. A wave of liquid light and love flowed into me. There was this explosion in my chest like streams of living water bursting forth from the depth of my soul.

I knew then—not just by faith, but because I had experienced Him—that God is real and God is love. My heart was filled with unspeakable joy, and I felt myself surrender my will to His will. Then it was as if His love and light visited every dark area of my soul. He went into every area of the house of my heart and opened every door and shined His light and then He did the same with every closet and every drawer. He touched me where all my failings and fears were and forgave me, healed me, and accepted me as His son.

Tears gushed from me unexpectedly. A cascade of joy and peace flowed within from the inside out. I raised my hands to the sky as if I were reaching right into heaven, and I heard myself exclaim, "Praise You, God. I love You, God." I was riding the perfect wave and I was one with that perfect wave. I was at one. I was at that still point. I had dropped in on a wave bigger and more powerful than I had ever dreamed of—right here in the middle of a dry and thirsty land. My only thought was that I wanted God to take me right then to heaven. Earth meant nothing to me. I did not want to live any longer on this earth; I just wanted to see Him face-to-face.

After that moment, nothing was the same. Colors seemed brighter, and regardless of my challenges, all I saw were hope and promise. I had found the perfect One and I was surfing that perfect wave of the Spirit. This was not happiness, because that depends on happenings. This was joy infused by God.

I would soon learn, though, that I couldn't stay on that particular wave for the rest of my life. I had yet to go to hell and back.

CHAPTER 5

Rite of Passage

1974–1983

Marty Brown and I cruised over the coastal mountains, having driven for more than twenty hours straight, and went right to the beach. Like me, he was an uprooted surfer from California transplanted by his parents to the heart of Texas. One night, we just packed up his little black VW bug and took off.

We pulled in on the north side of the jetty in Newport Beach at the infamous break called "The Wedge." It was big. It was ominous. No one was standing there saying, "You really missed it. You should have been here yesterday." At that time, The Wedge was considered the most dangerous surf spot in California. I would soon find that to be true.

There is no other wave in the world like The Wedge. When the swell is coming from the right direction it flows in and pushes at an angle to the big Newport Harbor jetty, then bounces off those rocks and heads back toward the beach at a right angle to the wave. This bounce-back wave causes an A-frame peak and doubles the size and power of the wave as it flies along the shoreline. It had not claimed any lives, but stories of battered bodies and more than one case of paralysis testified to its treacherousness.

The waves were breaking big and were breaking as perfect as I had ever seen. I knew that I would have to position myself in just the right place to catch the wave where that peak forms. There is a very real danger of being tossed up onto the jetty. I had heard a story of a rogue wave throwing a bunch of bodysurfers all the way over the jetty into the harbor. If I could swim out and avoid that catastrophe, then I would have still have to deal with by far the heaviest wave I had ever experienced.

I waited for a lull and swam out. I was nervous, but at that time in my life, I felt invincible in the water. As I swam hard to get past the impact zone, I realized that not putting on swim fins had been a bad idea. I dove as deep as I could and swam hard underwater so the wave would not suck me up its back and throw me out over the falls.

As I surfaced on the back side of the wave, I felt stronger currents than I had ever experienced before running through the lineup and pulling and then pushing me back and forth like I was in a washing machine. I determined to let the next set roll through and try to catch a smaller wave toward the end of the set. This turned out to be a bad idea.

In less than five minutes, a set started to peak up, and waves began to run along the jetty. It was now or never, so I went for the sixth wave of the set. It was one of the bigger waves, but I realized that it wanted to catch me whether I wanted to catch it or not. I swam as hard as I could, trying to get in early before the wave got too critical.

I soon realized that in spite of my efforts to get in early, it was going to be the latest and biggest drop of my life. I felt my body break loose from the grasp of the wave peak, and I began to slide—almost free-fall—down its hollow face. As I made the drop, I thought, *So this is how I'm going to die.*

I had been able to at least keep my feet dragging in the wave, and as I bounced and skidded along the surface, I extended the closed fist of my left arm as far out in front of me as I could and bent my knees to pull my weight forward. Then I began to drag my feet and use my extended hand as a forward rudder trying to direct myself down the line instead of straight down into the sandy pit. I traversed the face of the wave faster than I had ever surfed before and with the same sense of urgency that a skier has trying to outrun an avalanche. I was deep in the barrel, but I was stoked to realize that I was projecting myself sideways along the face of the wave parallel to the shore. I knew the farther down the line I got, the less power the wave would have. I would try to escape out the "doggie door" before it finally closed out on me.

The barrel spit me out with a fire hose of spray shooting me onto the open face. As I shook my head to clear the spray from my eyes, I could suddenly see why the other bodysurfers had chosen to go on the earlier waves. I saw a rip wave from one of the first few waves flying back at me from the beach. I knew it would make the wave face jack up, and that I would be tossed up and ragdolled. As it hit my wave, I went airborne. I spread my legs like a frog after it makes its jump, trying to regain traction somewhere on the wave, but there was no joy from that effort. So I tried to wrench my body and jackknife myself headfirst again down into the wave face.

Somehow, I landed back below the lip of the wave just about where I was before I had been tossed. Then, just as I began to traverse the face again, the bottom of the wave seemed to fall out. All I saw below me was sand boiling in about two feet of water. I was free-falling straight down its face into the grinding pit. Normally, I would just be able to tuck my head and somersault back under the force of the wave back out to sea, but the wave had ahold of me and there was nothing I could do.

I could already imagine my neck breaking. I arched my back and lifted my head as hard as I could, trying to plane out like a jet in a steep dive. Then a miracle happened. At the last millionth of a second before I thought I would feel my neck snap, a flood of water surged under my body and shot out in front of me on the shallow water below. Instead of cracking my neck, it split the new layer of water in half like the bow of a navy destroyer going at full throttle. I felt the wave sluicing by me on either side. I have never felt that feeling before or since. I finally leveled out and then was thrown up onto the steep, sandy bank. I grabbed sand so that the wave would not pull me back out to sea as it receded, and then clawed, crawled, and crab-walked my way up the beach. Then I ran as the next wave caught up with me and tried to kick out my legs.

I collapsed on the sand, with no thought of trying to look cool. I twisted around and looked out at The Wedge to see if it was coming for me again. I was alive, but more than that, I had lived. I laughed the deepest and loudest and happiest laugh of my life.

The surfers who ventured out here were real surfers, soul surfers. No wannabes, no posers. The Wedge separated the men from the boys. I did not know then that I would soon have to face that same divergence within my own soul.

Spiritually, I had paddled into beautiful, perfect, glassy waves with long open faces. It had been easy so far, and I presumed that it would always be that way. I thought that I had arrived. I was stoked. I was happy, but I was just a spoon-fed baby. After that experience at the prayer meeting, my spiritual journey did not require any great faith. God had made it easy for me. He had blown me away day by day with the experience of His presence. It required very little hope. What more could I hope for? It did not require love. I loved everyone. Of course, that was easy to say when there was nothing testing that love. It never even crossed my mind to consider that maybe I was more of a spiritual poser than I was a true soul surfer.

I had been experiencing a honeymoon with God. Sure, He was my Lord. Sure, He was my master. But that was easy, as I had had Him on *my* terms. This remained true until a great testing, a proving, a rite of passage, came into my life that was more challenging than the wave at The Wedge.

Increasingly, people around me started asking me the same question: Given the depth of my spiritual passion, was God calling me to be a priest? All of a sudden, I felt like I did in my Baylor English class, trying not to make eye contact with the professor as she looked for someone to diagram a sentence. I did not want God to call me out this way. Now when I prayed, "O Lord, I love You. You are my savior and my Lord," I could sense a response of "Oh really?" to that "my Lord" part. The wheels had come off the party bus.

I did not want to be a priest. I wanted to fall in love and have children. I'd been thinking about being a father for years. Within me was the power to create a whole new life, and for part of me to continue through that child. I had long ago begun to make decisions based upon what would be in the best interest of my future children.

Now here I was confronted: What if God wanted me to be a priest? The deepest part of me was crying out, "God, please don't make me do that. I want children. Besides, priests don't surf." (It turns out that they do, actually; I've since taught three of them to catch waves.) I was supposed to get my accounting degree, become a CPA, get married, have children, and live happily ever after.

Still, I hated the feeling of resisting God. I kept envisioning heel marks streaking along my spiritual path as God dragged me toward this inevitable detour in my plans. I had really liked the verse, "I know what I have in store for you; plans for peace not destruction; a future reserved for you full of hope. If you seek me I will let you find me" (see Jeremiah 29:11–13). But that was when I figured that God wanted me to do the cool stuff that I wanted to do. Now I wasn't so sure; I wasn't so ready and willing. Intellectually, I knew that if I accepted and followed God's plan, I would ultimately be stoked and happy. My heart was just not buying into it, though.

It was like I wanted to surf point breaks but instead God wanted me to surf beach breaks, or much worse: I wanted to longboard and He wanted me to shortboard. The more I struggled to resist, the deeper and deeper I found myself dug in. It was like trying to dig out a barb from the sea anemone we call *vanna* in Hawaii. The harder you try to pull it out, the deeper it goes. You have to just leave it alone and let it fester until it is rejected by the body and is pushed out. This barbed arrow from the Lord worked itself deeper into my heart and it festered and festered until my whole soul was sick.

I could no longer gaze back at Him who was gazing at me. I was a poser, a spiritual wannabe. I felt like those guys with the too-cool-for-school surf clothes who sit on the beach with the girls, acting like real surfers but who never get out past the shore break. I was more of a poser than the guy I had seen with his surfboard bolted permanently to the top of his car. I walked and talked like I was ready for prime time, but I had put a DO NOT DISTURB sign on the door of my heart.

I'll just harden my heart in this one area, I thought. *God can have all the rest.* What I found, though, was that if I hardened my heart in one area, my heart became hard in all areas—and not just toward God.

I knew that God wanted me to be His friend. He wanted me know Him in a genuine way. I had read about God's desire for friendship: "I will not call you servant anymore, for a servant does not know what the Father is doing. I will call you friends" (see John 15:15). I knew that to be truly in love is to be of one will. I knew that God is love and that being one with His will would be perfect love. That sounded cool to me, until I started to think about the implications: *You are my friends if you do what I command you.* What if I didn't want to do what He commanded me to do?

It was like He promised me the ocean but then took a detour through the desert. *Hey, wait a minute, God. Maybe You're not from around here. The surf is back that way.* But He trusted in me even if I did not trust in Him. He trusted that my love for Him was strong enough to be tested. He was not breaking my will. He was breaking the chains that imprisoned my will. My love was not perfected yet, for I feared that God had my best interests at heart.

I knew I was already too far into my soul surfari to turn back now. I couldn't turn back to the safety of shore—not after what I'd experienced from God. I knew I had to trust my will to His will, but in my heart, I felt like a child sitting in the corner pounding the ground and saying, "I don't want to. You're not the boss of me."

I had learned that to be double-minded was a very bad state of mind in big surf. This was big surf. I either had to totally commit and go for it and surrender all to Him or not. As Crazy Todd would say, "Go big or go home." Finally, I decided that something had to give. I resolved to fast for seven days and nights and then drive my 1971 yellow VW bug for fourteen hours up into the wilderness. I went to a young adult retreat at a Benedictine monastery in the

Sangre de Cristo Mountains of northern New Mexico. It was located in Holy Ghost Canyon, and had once been a hangout for the outlaw Billy the Kid. As I fasted, I asked God to show me His will and to give me the desire to do His will, to give me the "want to" to want to.

I arrived at the retreat center and they assigned me a roommate named Michael. I was exhausted, both from fasting and from the long drive, so I hit the sack early—but I just could not go to sleep. It was not the crisp mountain air and the light snow outside that kept me aware and awake; it was the battle within me. Then I heard Michael walk in and very quietly kneel by his bed and begin praying, "Lord, I love You and I give You my life."

This wasn't fair; I was being ganged up on. Finally, with a sigh of great relief, I prayed silently to the Lord, "As hard as it is to serve You, it is harder not to. I surrender my desire to have a family to You." I felt a sudden acceleration in my soul and a sudden releasing freedom like free-falling down the face of a wave. I had died to that vision for my life now and had given it to Him. But I still did not know if He wanted me to be a priest or not. Perhaps He would resurrect the vision of having children and give it back to me empowered by His blessings. Regardless, I wanted only His will now.

The next morning, we all entered the big mountain lodge retreat room with a crackling fire blazing in the hearth. I looked up and saw a beautiful woman. The very first thing that came to my mind was, *Could I be married to her and love her twenty years from now?* Something inside of me said, *Yes.*

I went up to meet her, and she told me her name was Sue. We spoke for a minute and then sat down for the retreat in big, soft leather cowboy rocking chairs. As we did, I said to her, "Have you ever met anyone you felt like you have known your whole life?"

I went back to Baylor, but Sue and I kept in touch. Six weeks later, I returned to New Mexico to visit a seminary and I hiked up a mountain next to it. I prayed up there for about an hour, asking God to make clear the path before me. Finally, I said, "God what do You want?"

Then, I sensed in the core of my being the answer: "Son, what do *you* want?"

"I want to be married," I said. "I want to have children."

With that, a verse came to me: "Delight yourself in the Lord and he will give you the desires of your heart" (Psalm 37:4 NIV). The certainty came to me that it was He who had planted that desire for family in my heart. I knew that I was free to be married and to be a father. He had given me that desire, and He would help me to realize that dream someday.

I got up with my spirits greatly lifted. I knew that I was

free to be married and to be a father. I was willing to do anything He wanted, and now I was glad to feel an assurance that I knew His will.

By holding on to nothing, I had gained everything. Just like that day at The Wedge, if I had sat scared on the beach watching the incredible surf, I would have been nothing more than a spiritual poser or a wannabe. Instead, I had dropped in.

It was game on. The dream was coming true. I graduated Baylor in December 1975 and desperately wanted to be as close to Sue as I could be. She was still two years away from her degree from New Mexico State University in Las Cruces. I moved out of the boiling humidity of Texas heat to the even hotter and sometimes sand-blown heat of Apache country, just a half mile from where Marty and I had gassed up as we made our surfari to The Wedge.

Three and a half years after we met, Sue and I got married. A few weeks before the wedding, though, she had a meltdown, literally breaking into hives. She confessed that she did not think she wanted to marry me. I was devastated. I was so in love with her, and I'd tied all my dreams to building a life together. With no reason to stay in New Mexico, I packed my car and decided to head west to the surf, but just before I left, Sue changed her mind and I stayed. Many years later, as things were falling apart between us, she told me she'd married me not so much for how much she loved me, but for how much I loved her.

All I knew at the time was that we were going to be married, and that a dream was coming true for me. The banners that preceded the wedding procession proclaimed, "The Spirit and the Bride say come" (see Revelation 22:17). Most of the members of our community in Las Cruces were quite poor, but they still showered us with cash gifts—so much so that we were able to make a down payment on a trailer home. Every Friday night thereafter, the sounds of drums, bongos, flutes, a dozen guitars, and a half dozen tambourines filled our home. The potluck dinners we had on Fridays were a godsend, as they provided a bit of variety to the rice-and-beans diet we maintained toward the end of each pay period.

I had just passed the CPA exam and, much to my amazement, Deloitte, one of the "Big 8" CPA firms, hired me. They hired from only the top 1 percent of the top schools in the world, but somehow they gave me a job. I would have to "dress for success." That meant dark suits, white shirt, and a power tie, which at the moment was red. I went to a men's store to buy two new suits that I could ill afford. While they were taking measurements to tailor the suit, Sue told me that she needed to make a quick call. A few minutes later, I walked to the counter to pay for the suits and Sue came up to me with a huge smile.

"We're pregnant," she said.

My dream had come true. I was stoked out of my mind. We were going to have a baby. Soon, though, a new reality set in. We had been married only four months. My wife was still in college, and suddenly a heavy sense of responsibility settled over me. A line from scripture popped into my head.

"Take up your cross daily and follow me."

I felt something in the very core of my being change forever as the weight of responsibility anchored me. Sue graduated from college one year after our wedding, and ten days later, our beautiful daughter Fawn was born. Sue stayed at home to care for our daughter and I soon discovered that the beautiful woman I was so in love with was an incredible mother, too. She seemed to know just how to care for our baby. I could hardly wait to get home each night to play with Fawn and see what new things she was doing. I was living my dream.

Still, having a child had an unexpected effect. Sue's focus turned almost entirely to our child and away from me. Our romance had begun to dim.

Since Sue had graduated, nothing was stopping us from fleeing the parched desert, and I badly needed to be around water. Since I'd moved away from the ocean six years earlier, I'd had the same dream every month or so. I would walk down to the edge of the cliffs at Seacliff Beach and look down to the bright blue gleaming water of the Pacific. Perfect waves rolled toward shore in endless sets. I would hurry down the one hundred fifty steps to the ocean below and run out to the shoreline to surf, but as I approached, the surf would go flat.

I put in for a transfer with Deloitte, but nothing opened up. However, Price Waterhouse, another Big 8 firm, wanted me—but the opening was in Minneapolis. While we were there interviewing, the land was beautifully green and lush with lakes and rivers everywhere. It was paradise compared to the arid desert. I did not realize then that our visit coincided with one of the four good weeks of weather Minnesota has every year. We were fooled and fell in love with it. We left the blistering heat of New Mexico for the blistering cold of Minnesota. Out of the frying pan and into the freezer.

My wife was pregnant again but we suffered a miscarriage. It was quite a hit for us to take. But a bit more than a year later, my oldest son Jeremiah was born. I was stoked. We had a son. But the pressure was on for more money.

"Take up your cross daily and follow me."

It was less than two years since I had made the move to the new company, but a new baby meant we needed more money. I was a hired gun ready to go to the highest bidder... again. I hired on with a Fortune 500 company, lowered my head like a fullback and worked my way up the corporate ladder, driven by the need for money for my family. I was working incredibly hard. I was keeping my family afloat. I was doing the responsible thing. I was doing the right thing, right? I remember looking out the window of my office as I approached my fourth winter in Minnesota. I watched as the last ducks departed from the private lake in front of our office that we all called the "indirect cost allocation pool."

The ducks got to go south for the winter. Not me.

I had become completely ensnared in the cares and worries of this world. I felt the way I did when, as a kid, I would get entangled in the seaweed monster in the shore break while wave after wave pummeled me. Instead of deepening my walk with God, I had neglected it. I was busy doing good things, but my times of communion with Him had become as short as the quick hugs with my wife as we passed in the hallway before I went off to work and she went to feed the babies.

Instead of spending time with God, I brought the same attitude to my life that I had when I played fullback in high school. I just lowered my head and ran over things. What I had begun in His power and grace I was continuing on in my own effort. I felt like a surfer who drops in on a big wave, turns, and then flies down the face only to find that he has outrun the power of the wave and is stalling and about to wipe out.

On top of this, a back injury I'd suffered in college carrying bricks had become chronic, and the pain was becoming increasingly debilitating. When I wasn't working, I would collapse on the couch. At times, I would miss a week of work because the pain was so bad I could not move.

Of course, none of this surprised God. He had a plan that He was intricately weaving into my life. Though I had been unfaithful, He was always faithful. He used all these challenges of life to allow me to dissipate my energy until I finally had no choice but to seek Him. While I slaved away, He rested. Looking back, I can sense He was saying to me, "You done yet? No? Okay, continue on as long as you like; I will be here. When you work I rest, but when you are finally exhausted in your own human strength and turn to Me, I will work."

I had moved for career and financial advancement so many times, but I'd gotten to the point where my only hope for promotion was if the person above me retired or died. I knew I needed to make another move, but this time I wanted it to be more meaningful. I missed the ocean and could not imagine raising our children in the cold.

I began playing Beach Boys music exclusively on the cassette player in my company car as I dreamed of surfing the warm beaches of Southern California. I felt like the Bear, the sage surfboard shaper in *Big Wednesday*: "Move inland. Live under a roof. Taxes, marriage…the whole damn thing." Now I wanted to return to my love, the ocean.

I could feel with each snowfall that something was dying inside me. It was brutally cold. I did not belong here.

I wanted to go to wherever ducks flew south. I could not flourish here, and I did not want my children living in the frozen tundra.

I remember coming home one evening and stepping into the house as quietly as I could. Back then, there always seemed to be a baby or a very tired mom sleeping. I quietly walked up the spiral staircase to our master bedroom. The fireplace in our room had a slow burn going, and my two wonderful children were beautifully, quietly asleep next to my wife on the bed. The TV was on with the sound turned low. On it was a film of surfers in Hawaii. Little did I know that I was looking through a time-warp window into my future, that the very people I was watching would be a big part of my life in the years to come.

Just as the surfers on the television were facing the huge challenges of enormous waves, I was facing huge challenges in my life. Unlike the surfers, though, I was trying to do so with too little power, because I'd been neglecting my prayer life and my time of communion with God. Instead of overcoming the challenges of life on God's power, I was going it alone at half throttle. I wasn't doing bad stuff. I was working hard for my family. But the coldest part of those winters was not just the cooling of my love affair with my wife (and it had gotten increasingly cooler now that there were two kids that kept her focus) but the coldness of my relationship with God. It was the time of the coldest winter swells I had ever experienced.

Then, one day as I headed to the corporate dining room, I felt moved to turn left and go outside for a walk. I heard a still, small voice say, "You are My walking man." From that day, I began a daily pattern of walking and praying that I still continue. At first, those walks were clouded with the cares and worries of the day, but in time my spirit rallied and my heart turned toward God. In that time, I found myself strengthened, encouraged, and refreshed in my sense of purpose. When I walked and prayed, a certain Zen came over me, a peacefulness, a moment of living in the now. As I walked, God would infuse me with contemplation; a very real sense of His presence or of inspiration, insight, or even a revelation. In time, I began to feel a sense of dialogue with God again, but it was deeper.

I started to realize that the closer I am to God, the simpler life becomes. That does not mean easier, just less complicated. Everything becomes clearer. How to live my life becomes more streamlined. All my ambitions and agendas fall away when I focus on God and the simplicity of just desiring to be in His presence.

As I became the "walking man" and renewed my prayer life, I sensed it was time for the Lord to open the door to returning to California. I found my heart settling on making a move west, but I could not make that happen. With a family of four and a single income, I could barely afford to take a Sunday drive much less start over on the West Coast.

Then suddenly a tailor-made job opportunity became available in warm Southern California. We had just moved into a brand-new home that we had built in a new development. It was perfect for our young family. With the weight of responsibility of raising the children, our marriage had been under increasing stress. Would Sue be willing to revive our lives in the revved-up world of California?

Her answer was a resounding, "NO!"

"What would it take," I asked her, "for you to be confident this was the right thing?" Her reaction was to storm out the door in tearful anger and drive away. About thirty minutes later, I loaded up the kids for a drive to get some much needed air. The thought came to mind that the atlas in our house did not show us clearly where Woodland Hills (the location of the possible new job) was, so I decided to go to the local library to use their maps.

The children and I found the reference section in the back of the library. The map I needed was not on the shelves, so I went ask for help. That's when I saw my wife sitting at a desk with the map spread out. She looked up at me, pointed her finger to a place on a map, smiled, and said, "Let's do it."

Thirty days later—during which the temperature never rose above freezing—we packed up yet another U-Haul.

Nearly every night during this wait, my recurring dream would come back to me, but with a new twist. I would stand above the ocean looking down the cliff at perfect surf and then I would run down the stairs to the water's edge. Now, though, instead of the surf going flat, I would surf all night in my sleep.

CHAPTER 6

Return to My First Love

1984–1987

The day after we arrived in California, we made our first trip to the beach. I'd practiced putting on my wetsuit at home, being sure the zipper was in back. I even tried on my new O'Neill split-toed booties. I had never worn anything but baggies in the water, so this gear was new for me. I'd hoped that I would look cool getting down to the water to begin paddling out, but even that was a fail. I had never worn an ankle leash before, and I ended up making the mistake of putting it on my front ankle instead of my back ankle.

I was stoked though. Thank God I was smart enough to buy the latest hot-blue-and-pink-sleeved wetsuit so I could be in style like all the other hot young shralpers, I thought. I did not want to look like an okie, a barney (as in barnacle), or a hodad. Here I am thirty years old and in my prime and

73

I am a cool surfer again. I made a little run into the shore break, but I tripped over my ankle leash, caught myself, and then twisted my ankle on some rocks hidden beneath the surface of the water. I planted myself headfirst into the seaweed. Pride comes before the fall, and no one takes more falls than a surfer.

My surfboard was four feet shorter than anything I had ever used before. Minnesota winters had added about six pounds a year to me, and I was tipping the scale at 220 pounds. I was a good forty-five pounds heavier than when I had last surfed. I pulled myself up prone on my board and felt it sink beneath me faster than the *Titanic.* I paddled hard, making my way through the cold January shore break and seaweed. Each wave brought with it a horrendous ice-cream headache, and I noticed that my hands were quickly tingling and numb. My arms were no longer trained for surfing, and I could hardly make it the short forty yards out to the lineup. I was accustomed to a longer board, so I had positioned myself too far back on this new shortboard, and the nose kept lifting as I paddled.

I finally got out to the lineup and looked around at the other surfers. They quickly looked away, not wanting to make eye contact with this thirty-year-old grommet. I paddled out a bit farther than everyone else, just trying to get my bearings, but soon learned why no one else was there. I was essentially in no-man's-land, halfway between the point break and the beach break. At least it looked like no wave would break there in the deeper water and I could catch my breath.

That's when the wave of the day took aim at me.

I felt like a scared young kid again as I paddled for the horizon while the wave approached. As I barely made it over the lip of the wave, its big brother roared down on me. It was a baptism by immersion. I rolled off my board and dove deep, grabbed on to some seaweed, and felt the wave tug at me as it passed over. I was laughing with joy the entire time, but then realized that laughing under water means you are not holding your breath.

It had been fourteen years since I had last paddled out. Now here I was back in the cool, refreshing, winter water of the Pacific. It was cold but not as cold as the blizzards I had left behind. I was sitting there ready to surf one of the spots I had been longingly listening to the Beach Boys sing about just a few weeks before: Ventura County Line, made famous by their song "Surfin' U.S.A."

I looked back to the shoreline. I saw fuel-efficient cars lined up along the Pacific Coast Highway and thought about how strange they seemed compared to my youth, when only a handful of muscle cars sat vigil as a few hardy souls surfed. It seemed that the attitude of everyone around me matched the flashiness of the neon colors of their boards and wetsuits. The noses of their boards were honed down and spear sharp; they seemed so strange compared to the rounded nose of the boards of my youth. As the beach girls' bikinis got smaller, their hair got bigger. Image replaced substance. Where were the soul surfers?

Hippie hair was replaced by hip hair and flowers painted on girls' nails were replaced by false nails. Aviator glasses were replaced by neon-rimmed mirrored lenses. When you spoke to someone there was always this annoying, distorted image of yourself in their lenses looking back at you. The single-fin boards of my youth were replaced by two-, three-, and even five-fin boards. It seemed even surfing had succumbed to the yuppie culture of more.

Soul had been supplanted by the "agro," go-for-it attitude and being stoked was replaced by selfish surfers taking every wave they could. Surfers were ripping the wave apart, not becoming one with it. Everything had changed so much. I felt like I was in a foreign land. Did I even belong here?

I turned my attention back out to the sea. Everything on land may change, but like God, the sea never changes. I looked out toward the point and then I saw two or three sage ones in dark wetsuits riding longer boards. I wondered where they got them. I had not seen any in the surf shops. They set out farther than the rest of the pack, and when one of the bigger waves came their way, they turned and paddled just two or three strokes and dropped in, surfing in long, drawn-out turns stalling their boards and cross-stepping to the nose to hang ten. They seemed like the real

Knights Templar seeking the Holy Grail, as I was. Not like most of the other surfers around me, who seemed more like the knights in the Monty Python film.

I had detached from the land. I had paddled out beyond the pack. It was just the sea and me. What lay before me was changeless. It was the same as it always was. The ocean, my love, had been waiting here for me patiently all this time. Something in me settled down, settled in, and felt so right.

I contemplated that although God is so dynamic and His creation reflects this, He is changeless. He is substance. He is the rock that does not move. In the midst of change, He is the constant. He is the eternal now.

I scanned the horizon for a wave. Unsteadily, I sat up on my small surfboard. I kept my center of gravity low, and leaned forward, clinging to both rails. I prayed, "Oh God, how deep, how wide, how unchanging is Your everlasting love." I raised my hands ever so slightly in a moment of praise. It would have been an intensely spiritual moment, except that my actions had caused my weight to shift, and I rolled sideways and fell off my board.

Humbled, I crawled back on my board and turned my attention to riding a wave. I waited on the shoulder, too intimidated to go to the peak. This meant that the only way I was going to get a wave was if everyone else missed it, or one of the riders fell. I would paddle hard in case a surfer would fall, but then he would make a run at me, making a slashing turn at the last moment as I backed out, throwing a cold spray of water in my face. These surfers were making a very clear statement: "Hodad, go home!" I knew in my heart, though, that I *was* home.

Then I saw my chance. A wave came as if it was meant just for me. I paddled with all my might, dipping my hands deep into the fifty-five-degree water, and felt the familiar rush of the wave catching me. Now, I was racing down the face of the wave. Everything was fine, except I could not get up. The board wobbled as I tried to stand. I had my butt up and my hands and feet glued to the board. It was ugly and getting uglier. Finally, I pushed myself up, got to my feet—and then moonwalked backward off the board.

The "hot" surfers made it look so easy, but all through that day and into the weeks ahead, I seemed to be perfecting my downward dog yoga move, followed by the backward moonwalk. I realized that my fullback frame was simply not working on these smaller boards. I needed to find a longer board, but no one seemed to make them anymore.

That's when providence intervened.

A new family moved in across the street with surfboards in the back of their truck. We connected immediately, and Howard, the husband, and I dawn-patrol-surfed the next morning, with me achieving the usual results.

"You know," Howard said, "I have an old longboard you could use." It turned out he'd left it at his old home, plan-

ning to abandon it. It was the ugliest surfboard I had ever
seen. It had snail tracks all over the top and bottom of it and
the fiberglass had been covered with white marine paint.
The single glassed-in fin was not exactly glassed-in anymore; it wobbled when you touched it.

"No worries," Howard said. "Duct tape will take care of
that." This was my introduction to duct tape as the miracle
cure for all that ails a surfer. For the first years of my surfing
rebirth, I had at least one piece of duct tape somewhere on
my board. I became such a big fan of duct tape that, when
I finally got a new board, I told my shaper to airbrush fake
duct tape on it and to inscribe TEAM DUCT TAPE on the
bottom.

The next morning, Howard and I loaded up the boards
and headed back to County Line. The board must have
weighed thirty-five pounds; it listed to one side. It had
become waterlogged from being sprayed daily by the ubiq-
uitous California sprinkler system. I pulled it off the truck
and worked my way down the rocky slope to the beach,
being careful not to hurt any of the rocks with it.

I put on my leash, walked out to the shore break, plopped
the board on the water, jumped on it, and started to knee-
paddle out. *This feels right*, I thought. You can't knee-paddle
on a short board. When I got out to the lineup, the other
surfers eased away from me. Their pristine, airbrushed
neon-bright little boards were in grave danger of the Big

Kahuna, as my board came to be known. I felt like a fullback again, ready to lower my head and go full speed ahead.

The first wave came and I paddled for it. The board did not want to move at first, but with every stroke, it gained speed. I slid down the slope of the wave and stood up. There was no downward dog, no face planting, and no moonwalking off the back this time. I felt myself beginning to fall, but then the board slid under my center of gravity and I rode straight ahead.

I saw fear in the bulging eyes of the other surfers as expletives exploded from their mouths and they dove off their boards to avoid me. Was it wrong that I took a certain joy in this as I reflected on all the times their hard cutbacks had sprayed my face?

The loose fin vibrated and became looser as my speed increased, but I was riding through the shore break. I stepped off the board into the shallow water and bowed to my wife, who was on the beach pretending not to know me. I had just surfed my first wave in fourteen years, and I felt more alive than I could ever remember being.

A few weeks later, Sue told me she was pregnant again. My son Shane was about to explode in all his power and energy onto the scene. We certainly wanted another child— Fawn and Jeremiah had brought us so much joy—but at the same time, I couldn't help hearing His words.

"Take up your cross daily and follow me."

I knew we were tapped out financially and that I had no hope for a pay raise in my current position. Meanwhile, my job ended up requiring me to fly to the East Coast three out of four weeks and then work my way back to the West Coast calling on the largest banks in the country. With my travel came taking clients out to eat two or three times a day. As stressed as I was feeling when I wasn't in the ocean, it was hard to push back from the table, and I gained more weight. The extra weight added to my back problem, and my back problem caused me not to exercise as much, which caused me to gain even more weight. I found myself going from glad Dad to mad Dad easily.

My family needed money. I had to make a move. Soon after, a major New York bank hired me as an assistant VP to represent them on the West Coast. The only thing that mattered to me was that the job came with a company car, a substantial pay raise, and a lot less travel. I needed to feed my family. I was a mercenary. I was a gun for hire. *Just show me the money.* Job satisfaction was meaningless to me.

My "walking man" breakthrough felt like a distant memory now. I had less and less of a sense of intimacy with God, but I found myself driving in the company Cadillac saying, "God, I need a sabbatical." I had been working my butt off since I was thirteen with no more than a week or two of vacation. I needed a break or I was going to snap.

The break came in an unexpected way. The bank decided

to centralize its Southern California operations back to New York, and they asked me if I was ready to go east.

"Let me think about it," I responded. "NO!"

They gave us more of a silver streamer than a golden parachute. As I headed out of the downtown L.A. office that morning driving my big company Cadillac, I was a scared and worried man. "God, what did I do wrong?" We had three children now. They had given me only four months of severance pay. What was I going to do?

I drove straight to the ocean in Santa Monica and then up along the beach on the Pacific Coast Highway. I cruised past Malibu. It was a bright, beautiful day. As I made my turn to drive up through the beautiful Malibu canyon, something in my soul turned. A sense of adventure replaced my trepidation, and by God's grace I was able to turn my worry into praise. I realized that God is not surprised by anything. This was a chance to exercise my faith. I was going to get to watch God work. Me plus God would always win no matter what the circumstances. The biggest, ugliest set of my life was rolling toward me out of the fog, and instead of running for cover I turned and paddled into the wave of my future.

In my youth I was always surprised by setbacks and adversity. Now I thought of challenges and tribulation as the norm and it was only my attitude toward them that I could control. A thought came to mind just then: *These next months may be the gnarliest yet, but no matter how challenging, God will lead me through it and His will will be done.* He would use these circumstances to teach me and to transform me in ways I could not without them. I would abandon myself to the wildness of His will.

I felt a surge of God through me. My head lifted and I knew I just had to go hide out with God. I did not need a road map. I just trusted Him that I would hear His voice tell me where to place my next step. Nothing ever comes as a surprise to Him. I was out of work and stoked. I got home with a spring in my step for the first time in months. Since it was the middle of the day, my wife was surprised to see me.

"Honey what are you doing home so early?"

"I got fired! Are you ready for the next adventure?"

She looked at me, a baby in one arm, Fawn playing with her Barbie dolls at our feet, and Jeremiah trying to crawl up me like I was a tree.

"What are we going to do?" she said.

"I don't know, but this is the best thing that could possibly happen to us. It's too big of a challenge for me to handle, so I guess it's up to God. Only God knows what's around the corner."

Six weeks later, I found myself rested, refreshed and reenergized in my spirit, soul, and body. I had taken the opportunity to go to the beach every day and read through the New Testament, the Old Testament, and then the New Testament again and had seen the common thread of God inviting us, challenging us to enter into His land of rest.

I had begun to feel a strong sense that I should start my own CPA firm. I was ready to get to work. I was overqualified for all the positions that came my way and I just had this feeling of not wanting to be a square peg in a round hole anymore. I wanted something that would challenge me, cause me to stretch my wings, and that would most of all be fulfilling. I had always sold myself to the highest bidder just to provide for my family.

I could never have dreamed of leaving a good job to start my own firm; it would've been too much of a risk and a burden to put on my family. But God had put me in a position where I really had no choice. I smiled upward. *Thanks, God; Your plan is better than mine.* I broached the subject with Sue.

"Do it," she said. "We're going to need it. We're pregnant again."

I should have been shocked because she'd had had her tubes tied, something her mother had talked her into. However, when she went for the operation, we prayed together: "Lord if it is Your will for us to have more children do not let this operation work." Not long before she had given me this news, I woke up in the middle of the night and awakened her. "Honey," I said, "we made a baby last night, and his name is Joshua."

He was born on the first day of my first tax season.

His words played again in the recesses of my soul: *Take up your cross daily and follow me.* But this time, somehow, the burden seemed lighter.

7

Wave of Healing

1987–1991

I could hear the explosive sound of boulders crashing into each other as the huge surf tossed them around like beach balls. I worried that my foot or leash might get caught under one of them, causing me to drown. Howard and I had launched out to sea, paddling for what seemed like forty minutes, struggling with the current and trying to duck under the relentless oncoming waves. The farther out I got, the bigger the sets broke. It was the biggest swell I'd ever seen in my life, and it was still building.

This was Rincon, which means "point" in Spanish. It was a point break, meaning there was no deep-water paddling channel to break out through. Finally, there was a lull, and I paddled for the horizon in an all-or-nothing effort, tapping every ounce of strength and wave knowledge that I had left in me. As it turned out, the lull was simply the ocean storing up energy for the biggest set of the day—and there I was in no-man's-land. I saw Howard just make it over the face, but I was too far inside. I was not going to be as fortunate.

I had to turn and take the death drop.

I made a few strokes toward shore, which was several hundred yards away. I called out "Jesus!" and caught a deep breath as the heaviest wave I had ever experienced exploded on the back of my board, launched me up and toward shore, and then covered me in a wall of white water. I held my breath and grabbed on to the board for dear life as I rocketed for long seconds toward the bouldered cliff less than a quarter of a mile ahead, expecting it to shatter both my board and me.

Suddenly, I shot out from the water. I sucked in a deep, life-giving breath, just missing a wild-eyed surfer as I came out of the liquid cannon. I saw the thirty-foot seacliff along the Pacific Coast Highway was just fifty yards in front of me. I rolled off the board, trying to get under the foam bubble of water to have it cushion me. This worked almost too well. The water below me got caught up in the rip from the wave in front of me, rolling back out to sea. I realized that I would not get crushed on the boulders, but I would instead be sucked back out to sea to go through the rinse cycle all over again. I dove deep and swam as hard as I could, trying to get to the sea cliff. Finally, I felt my hand grab a boulder and then I pulled my other hand against the tide and held on to another rock for dear life like an *opihi*, or mussel.

I pulled myself closer, regripping with my left arm to cling to the cliff. While holding my breath, I reached down and undid my board leash from my ankle and held on to it. I realized that my board could end up being the death of me if that wave sucked it back out to sea with me still tied to it.

It is useless to fight a wave like this. Up to that moment, I had always felt invincible in the water. But now it had become an unpredictable wild animal. I had experienced a similar feeling of awe and trepidation less than a year earlier when I had been surfing at Refugio, an hour north of where I was at the moment. There is deep water just off the point there, so whales often cruise close to the beach. I was the only surfer out at the point. As I rested easy, waiting for the next set and the approaching sunset, I felt an upwelling beneath me like a rising wave, except that no wave was approaching. Suddenly, a massive body slowly rose next to me. I found myself glancing into the fist-size eye of a gray whale.

I was stoked beyond belief, but I was also very aware that this was a wild animal capable of anything. My instant concern was that my leash would somehow become entangled with the whale, and if it dove deep, it would unwittingly kill me. I slowly reached under the water, not wanting the whale to become wary of my movements, and undid my leash.

People don't call whales and dolphins "animals." We

instinctively call them "creatures," for with that word we intimate that they are a reflection of their awesome "creator." I dipped my hand on the far side of my board and slowly and gently paddled closer to the whale. I only needed to get eighteen inches closer to reach out and touch it. I don't know how such a massive creature could make such an imperceptibly delicate swimming motion, but no matter how much I paddled, our distance stayed the same. At the same time, the whale did not move farther away. It was a sublime contemplation of two alien beings from separate worlds brought together by the sea.

We sat like that for long minutes and then, as the sun began to kiss the horizon, the whale slipped beneath the waves and was gone. Those moments when we were together imparted a timeless, reckless, ecstatic, exhilarating feeling to me that has never left me and reminded me of the fearful wildness of God that would not tolerate anything but complete freedom from me.

And now, here I was in Rincon, clinging for my life against the raging sea, which, unlike that other wild animal, had turned on me. I was holding my breath and my leash as wave after wave of the biggest set of the day crushed me. I had just enough time to suck in oxygen and hold on tighter before the next wave rolled over me and then tried to rip me off the rock as it receded.

Finally, the last massive wave cascaded over the top of me,

and I made a scramble for freedom, clawing my way up the cliff, oblivious to any cuts or bruises as I dragged my board behind me. I was not worrying about the massive dings I was probably inflicting on my board, either. I just wanted to live. I ran up the cliff face, dragging the board behind me, willingly damaging it in exchange for my life. I reached up and grabbed the last boulder, and as I did hands reached down, grabbed my wetsuit, and pulled me up onto the four-lane highway above. Only then did I see all the cars that had stopped and all the people that lined the cliff watching the sight of these huge waves that exploded on the cliff and splashed water halfway across the four-lane highway.

Someday in heaven I want to meet the angel that saved me that day at Rincon. He is one very busy, very good swimmer.

At that moment, the big surf was destroying the massive, twenty-foot-high Ventura Pier just a few miles away. It ripped apart huge planks and then just splintered the supporting structure. I turned, sat down, and looked out to sea, so glad to be alive. The first thing I had thought as the waves started barreling down on me was my children and who would take care of them. I learned that you can't be thinking thoughts like that in big surf. You can't have anything in your mind that makes you hesitate.

I felt totally and completely humbled and clean. I was emptied of any pride or arrogance. It was replaced by reliance on God and respect for His awesomeness as reflected by His creation. I had gone on a journey to the very extent of my endurance and ability. I had in a sense plumbed the depths of my soul, and I came to understand clearly that I was a finite being with very definite limits. I had a new-found fear and respect for the ocean and for its Creator. And I had a respect for myself as well. I felt fully humbled and fully alive. That is the abundance of life that God promises us—from sorrow to joy, from fear to empowerment.

In some ways, I felt closer to the ocean than I ever had, for the ocean had my life in her hands and chose to let me live. I had gone on a journey to the very extent of my endurance and ability. The ocean is not a Disneyland ride, and I had learned to respect it. The beginning of understanding must start with fear. From that point, I learned to respect myself and my own wave skills and wave knowledge as both good and bad experiences built up my *manna* and *manao*. It's important to know your limits, but to always push them one step at a time.

People often ask me, "When you ride those big waves, or do some of the other crazy things that you do, do you have a death wish or something?"

My response is that it is quite the contrary. People who take the kinds of risks I do are the most safety-conscious people I know. We don't have a desire to die, but rather a tremendous desire to truly live. If I jump out of a plane, I make sure I have a reserve chute that is inspected. I know that I have an altimeter device that will automatically deploy my canopy if I have not opened it when I get to two thousand feet. When I learned to pilot a plane, a big part of the focus was on learning how to handle everything that could go wrong and what to do about it. We practiced putting the plane in a stall and recovering. Before I fly, I complete a step-by-step inspection and procedure checklist before taking off and landing.

If I want to surf big surf, I have to train months ahead of time by running in the sand, distance paddling, and diving deep and holding my breath. At times, I will hitchhike a ride on the catamarans that sail off from the shores of Waikiki. I will ride with them way out beyond the reef and then dive in and swim back to shore.

The Hawaiians have a tradition I try to follow. At sunset, as the sun hits the water, I take a deep breath and pray softly as I slowly let my breath out. I try to let out my last breath as the sun gives off a bluish green flash and sinks beneath the waves. If you can do that, you can begin to feel better about going out in big surf, but you will never feel at ease.

Every year, I take on a new physical challenge. These challenges tend to work on my spirit from the outside in and from the inside out. It is good to train our souls to be powerful so that when adversity comes we are up to the challenge and we are not surprised. One year I may take a black-belt test, the next year paddle my surfboard on a distance challenge. My most recent failure was at kitesurfing. It's the most refreshing, fun, and exhilarating feeling in the world to fail. Chuck Inman, whom I taught to tandem-surf and who is now a world champion, is my personal trainer. He challenges me to keep lifting weights to the point of total muscle failure. Only by pushing oneself to the point of failure can you truly get strong.

Man is wired with a thirst to live life to the fullest. We eventually discover that the only thing that can quench that thirst is the very wellspring of God that He has given us access to in our spirit—the deepest part of our being where "deep calls to deep as the waters roar" (see Psalm 42:7). It is in this deepest of places, when and where we come to an end of ourselves, that we can reach down and unfasten the leash that clings to our false securities and where we can come eyeball to eyeball with the wildness of God Himself. Our only peace is to undo our leash and cling to Him.

I went home that day from Rincon feeling more open to possibilities and more alive than I had ever felt in my life. He had promised me abundant life. He did not say it would be an easy life. He did not say He would take out the highs and lows, but that He would be with me. It supercharged me as I carried the weight of providing for my family and the challenge of facing my first tax season. I was on the verge of going underwater financially, and I was definitely in over my head trying to understand the new tax law. For the next hundred days, I sat frozen in my chair working longer hours than I ever thought I could. Somehow, I survived, but sitting in the same position for so long had put my back into a constant spasm.

The giant winter surf had come and gone with the first tax season of my new firm. Flowers were blooming, the Dodgers were playing baseball, and it was time for me to come out of winter hibernation. I hoped I could get my back loosened up a bit and drop the tax season weight I'd gained. At that point, my back went out completely. I was terrified and I wondered if I would ever get out of bed again.

I went to a back specialist, who referred me for a second opinion to another doctor, who in turn referred me to the UCLA Medical Center, to a world-renowned, well-published back researcher and surgeon. Every test this surgeon ran revealed nothing. He brought it before a committee of doctors for their thoughts, and they were stumped. They had no idea why I was in so much pain. They sent me out for therapy, and that immediately resulted in spending weeks in agony on my bed.

I had been prayed over several times by friends and family. I even went to one of those hyped-up healing evangelists, but that felt wrong from the start. The evangelist told me that if I had enough faith, I would be healed. That made no sense to me. I couldn't push God around like that and make Him do whatever I wanted. I knew that God was not a spiritual vending machine.

The evangelist seemed to be talking about faith in faith,

not faith in God. He said I needed to try hard to believe, as if white-knuckling it would impress God. But what he was talking about did not seem like the resting, trustful way that God had been teaching me. It seemed more like presumption than faith. Friends and family had prayed over me many times but nothing improved. I rested my trust in Him, hoping for a healing while my pain increased and my condition worsened.

I had no doubt that the one who sent those huge waves was certainly powerful enough to heal me at any time He wanted. But, did He want to? I knew that suffering was as real a part of any true walk with the Lord as was the joy that sustained me through it. He never said, "Sign up with Me and I will make your challenges go away." Trust in the midst of our challenges—that is what makes magic happen and when we get a glimpse at the power and wisdom of God. If He suffered, I had to be willing to suffer and join Him in it.

That summer, I decided to take a theology class on Signs and Wonders. There were a couple hundred of us in the room. I was in a lot of pain, so I sat in the back so I could easily slip outside and stretch on the grass if I needed to.

The music was beautiful, and the praise expressed there seemed transparent and real. It brought me back to the days in New Mexico when we just surfed through worship, letting God send His waves. It was clean, free from any emotionalism or feeling of manipulation. After each class, there was lab time, just like we had in chemistry class in college.

The teacher would leave the room and leave the microphone open, giving a wide berth to whatever God wanted to do.

At one break like this, someone walked up to the microphone and said that he sensed that God wanted to heal someone of a back problem. This caught my attention, but I figured that everyone had some sort of back pain.

"He hurt himself carrying bricks."

At that moment, I felt as though another tsunami hit me. I felt an infilling in my soul and body. I knew God was doing "stuff," and I began to thank Him quietly. My back pain subsided, but only a bit. The person who had spoken earlier asked if anyone felt that these words were for him. I raised my hand, and they directed me to a side room.

I respected that. This was no circus sideshow. They would not make a spectacle out of me. I went to the room, and the people there prayed for me. It reminded me of the bedroom where I had been prayed over in Texas when God first filled me. It was in gentleness and peace that they prayed for me, and it was obvious to all of us that something was happening. I felt God doing more "stuff," but I felt no significant improvement. Though the pain remained, I could feel something had changed and that the root physical cause had been healed and that the residue of pain and inflammation would soon subside. So I just rested in my healing. I had done nothing to cause my healing, and certainly nothing to deserve it other than to just trust in His perfect will.

Within a matter of days, the pain was completely gone and has never returned.

I knew that I had been in a lot of pain, but I had no idea how much until it was gone. For thirteen years, I had lived in paralyzing agony. With my healing came a dramatic change in my energy level and my emotional disposition. I could surf all day. I could hike all day, and even run. All without agony. I did not know then how important my back would be to my future endeavors in surfing. People always say to me, "You must have a powerful back to lift a woman over your head while you surf." I always respond, "Oh, that isn't me, that's God."

I am more aware of God's power than I was of the power of those waves that exploded on me as I clung to the rocks that day at Rincon. My back healing reminds me moment by moment that when I am weak, then I am strong, for it is not by might, not by power, but by His spirit that I can even surf. I have learned that when I have come to the very end of my own efforts, God is there waiting, saying something like, "Do you want to learn to move in My power or keep going on your own strength alone? Are you ready to ride the waves of the Spirit?"

It was the time of the summer swell and God had sent His healing waves.

CHAPTER 8

The Great Wipeout

1990–1995

I was in a fury. I was in a furious liberating rage. Anyone who wanted to live would probably not surf the eight-to-ten-foot shore pound that greeted me as I pulled up to County Line. The previous winter's swell had dredged all the sand from the beach and dumped it hundreds of yards out to sea. The beach lay as scarred and exposed as my soul. There was no sand, only rocks as the waves broke on just a few feet of water almost right up to the boulders that lined the ten-foot cliff below the Pacific Coast Highway. As I drove down to the beach, the CD player blasted out the words, *"Set me free, why don't you, babe? Get out of my life, why don't you, babe?"* so loud that one speaker broke and my ears rang.

It had taken me only fifteen minutes to make the twenty-five-minute drive. Only the ocean could save me. She was the only one I could trust anymore. She would understand my rage. She would be faithful to me. I could always count on her to accept me in any state I was in.

It was high tide, but it was the lowest point in my life. The A-frame peaks rolled in fast in seemingly unridable hollow tubes as they built and built and finally tripped up and broke on the bouldered shoreline. Each wave sucked up a truckload of sand. They were huge. They were ugly. They were unridable.

They were me.

Cowboy Dave was there next to his pickup, but as I jumped out of my Jeep Cherokee, he did not throw me his usual big grin. He saw the state I was in and said nothing to me as I pulled on my wetsuit, grabbed my board, not bothering to put my surf leash on it, and jumped down from boulder to boulder to get to the water's edge.

I paddled straight out into the impact zone, not waiting to time the sets. I didn't care if I took a direct hit from an oncoming wave. Somehow, my board survived the onslaught. In just a few strokes I was past the shore pound and out in the lineup. I had never seen County Line look anything like this. Its rage mirrored mine.

I was on my custom-made nine-foot-three Jacobs. It was my steed. I had watched it being shaped in my shaper's barn the same way a rancher watches a new colt enter the world. It was the best, most responsive board I had ever ridden. I felt that it was alive, and today it was as if it sensed my fierceness the way a horse senses a warrior's fire before battle. We were of one mind, the board and me, and it would not let me down. The next wave towered toward me, blocking out the late-afternoon sun. I turned at the last minute, took four strokes, and dropped in.

There was no way I could make this wave but I decided to make it really impossible by paddling with my fin in front. I jumped up as the board dropped in. As the fin dug into the wave face below me, I grabbed my right rail and looked way to my right, torqueing my body to make the board spin 240 degrees to put the nose of the board in front. Then the wave torpedoed me in a sudden acceleration down the line. I tucked down deep on my board and tucked deep in the wave, grabbing my right rail and leaning into the wave as I shot along its face for no longer than it takes a lightning bolt to scorch the sky. I was deep in the wave as the sand mixed with water and screamed an echoing freight train howl at me from within its bowels.

I was swallowed up and pounded to the sand beneath me. I should have let go of my board and let it fly toward the shore, but instead I stayed with it until the wave, like Jonah's whale, finally spit us out, ejecting us on the sand. I felt that my ribs would crack and I wanted them to. I wanted my emotional pain to morph into physical pain, so I could wrestle it to the ground.

I grabbed my board quickly, spun, and paddled back out to sea so fast that I was able to catch the same wave that I had just ridden in as it ripped back out to sea. It rocketed me through the impact zone and back out to the lineup almost effortlessly.

Wave after wave, I dropped in fin first and then helicoptered my board, spinning it in a tight death spiral. Each time I blasted down the line, I was swallowed up and pounded so severely, so deep in the wave, that each time I came out I was amazed that I was not dead. I was surfing better than I ever had in my life. *At least*, I thought, *I'll go out in a blaze of glory.*

The sun had set and the night was coming on when finally, mercifully, in the depth of a closeout barrel, I felt my board buckle, snap, and then split in half. As the wave spit me and the two pieces of my board out onto the sand, I looked up toward the Pacific Coast Highway and saw Cowboy Dave standing guard. He had stepped out of his Levi's and boots and back into his surf trunks, just he and my very busy guardian angel watching over me.

My board had given to me all it had, like a great steed that finally breathes its last at the end of an epic battle. I put the two ends of the board together; it was a clean break. I could have had the board repaired, but it wasn't meant to be that way.

Cowboy Dave called down to me as I walked toward him. "You must have really needed that."

"It was necessary."

I began to climb up, but he stopped me. He reached into the back of his truck and threw me a lighter and lighter fluid. "Go finish it."

I knew what I had to do. I walked along the rocky shoreline, stepping from boulder to boulder at high tide, around the point and out of the view of the Pacific Coast Highway, with two pieces of my board in one hand, and the makings of a fire in the other.

I sat the two pieces of board against a big piece of driftwood, making a chimney, then gathered sticks and some manzanita bark. I poured whatever was left in that can of lighter fluid on my board, stepping back to the water's edge, prepared to dive in if the heat got too intense. I lit the two pieces of my board, and they exploded in a blaze that lasted a good two minutes, but then quickly dissipated. The outer resin had burned rapidly, but the inner foam core just smoldered. I felt the same way.

The fire of rage within my soul had finally been liberated and flamed out, but I smoldered now in the core of my being, with naked pain. The pain now, without the protective coating of rage, was fully exposed. As I walked back to my Jeep, a cop was searching the point with his flashlight. Someone must have reported the fire. I signaled to him that it was okay and he drove off.

But it wasn't okay. I stood by my Jeep as the cold finally

crept into my consciousness. I had liberated the fury that had been building up inside me for a hundred days. The rage in my chest had broken free and was gone, but now it had been replaced by a painful fist-size lump in my throat that was like a dam holding back my tears.

I went back to my empty house. My wife was gone, my children were gone, and my dreams were gone.

The night before the start of the tax season, Sue had surprised me by asking me out on a date. It had been a long time since she had been interested in doing anything with me, so I saw this as a hopeful development. As the Chinese food arrived, though, she simply said, "I'm leaving you." I realize now that she must have wanted to tell me in a public place so I had to control my pain and anger as she broke me with her news.

On the surface, I had done everything right. I was a good man and a good provider. I had only been drunk once in my life, never smoked weed, and never took any drugs. I gave money to charity, paid my taxes, and even helped coach my kids' football teams. I had high expectations for myself, but part of the problem was that I had high expectations for everyone else around me, too—especially my wife and children. How many times had I been short with them? How often had I let the choking cares and worries of the world strangle me with so much pressure that I was not the father they needed me to be? I valued passion but forgot about compassion. To leave me was probably the bravest thing Sue had ever done and perhaps the wisest. We were like oil and water, different in every way except for our love of God. She had to do it for her own sanity and peace of mind.

I was a hypocrite. I was no man of God. I was a poser, a wannabe.

I realized that my rage was not so much for what I had lost in losing my wife; realistically, I had lost that long ago. It was because I had been holding on to the dream for my children to experience a stable home environment. We had just moved into a new home in the nicest and newest neighborhood in town. We had kept the old house as a rental. I had just earned my first-degree ninja black belt and my master's degree in taxation. My accounting firm was thriving, and for the first time in my life I was financially ahead and did not have to worry about how to make the next house payment.

Recently, we had even bought eight acres on the border of Glacier Park in Montana, just four miles from Canada. I had this idea that it would be fun and a good workout to build a small wood-frame hunter's cabin by myself, but it turned out that I was no better at building a foundation for our cabin than I had been at building a foundation for our family.

In the months leading up to Sue's announcement, I had been hearing words repeated in my soul in the same place that I sensed God's voice. "All that can be shaken will be shaken. All that can be taken will be taken. All that can be burned will be burned." I did not hear these words with a sense of fear or dread. I just had a certainty that a great shaking was coming into my life to sort things out, to put things in their right place. God was sending me a clear signal, a warning before a great storm surf roared into my life. The warning let me know to not try to fight it. I knew that after this coming storm surge, God would be there, and there would be a new beginning.

I had no idea how completely everything in my life would be swept away by this tide and how horrific this onslaught would be. I had hoped that the shaking would just be a new spiritual truth that God wanted to teach me—but this was to be as real as a bullet flying at my heart. My wife, my two youngest kids, and even my dog were gone. Sue had packed up a U-Haul, loaded up the brood, and headed back to her parents' home in New Mexico.

At the end of the summer, my sons returned, but Sue did not. Fawn had journeyed out on her own pilgrimage to the surf of Hawaii and then back to the mountains on her own search for healing. Each night, I would put the two boys to bed and then slip out into the mountains, wanting to cover myself with the night. In the mountains, I could turn my thoughts toward the pain and just sink into it. It was the dark night of my soul. I would cry out to God for comfort, though I knew there would be no answer. Why would He console someone who had failed Him so? I would hike the narrow dusty trail down to a small dried creek under a California oak and then up beyond a small rise, until I was completely alone in the dark.

Just my pain and me.

I came to know the sounds and feelings of the night. As I crossed certain terrain, I would feel the cooling river of air cascade down from the mouth of a narrowing canyon. I came to know a particular owl that always made a run past me from a distant tree. At first, I had the romantic notion that the owl and I were experiencing the beauty of the night together, but I soon realized that I was just his hunting dog, stirring up small animals that he could pounce on for a late-night snack.

The land around me was alive with the hunters and the hunted, and it felt so much like my life. I heard the call of the coyotes as they cried out to each other from canyon to canyon and then would hear them as they gathered in hot pursuit of their prey. I never knew a rabbit had a voice, but I heard its forlorn screams for help and mercy, and in that sound heard the pain of my own children as the devastation of the divorce showed them no mercy and no relief. Then I heard the howls of delight as the coyotes tore the defenseless creature apart.

Night after night I hiked, and the months slowly passed until a full year had gone by since my surf rage at County

Line. The nights in the mountains allowed me to go deeper and deeper into the pain, but still there was no relief. The dam just would not break. No tears would come.

Sue came back to finalize our court paperwork, and she stunned me by suing for full custody. She wanted to take my children to New Mexico. I had wanted her to return to California and live close so they could still have both parents nearby, but she was determined to pirate them away.

I felt as though I had been kicked in the gut. My kids were staying with her in a motel, so I headed for the solace of my mountains. I was the walking man, and I walked into the night toward the dry creek. This time, though, everything was out of focus. I reached up to rub my eyes to try to clear them, and found my hands were wet with tears. Then I realized I was lying flat on my face, spread out on the dirt. I grabbed at the dirt and willed my soul to break and for the pain to be fully released.

And then, it did. The dam broke and tears gushed out.

I howled in the night. The dark night of my soul had finally reached midnight. All the pain that had been stored up through my whole life flooded out—all the awkward fears and rejections of my youth, all the betrayals, all the loneliness, all the pain of dreams lost, the pain of never living up to my own expectations, the pain of failing as a father and a husband, the pain of failing God. All the pain in my life exploded in a crescendo of tears and pooled in the dirt below me.

An hour or more must have passed and finally the flood subsided. I had believed in God's unconditional love, but I felt that I had been especially blessed by the Lord and yet had denied Him and betrayed His kindness by failing so miserably in every possible way. I who had been so blessed, how could I expect anything from Him but condemnation? I who had been so wrongfully full of expectations for my wife and children, how could I now expect any affection or consolation from God?

Then finally I discovered the seed of the simplest of all truths: that God looked past my faults and saw my wounds and my needs. He accepted me as I was but then reached down to heal and by His grace alone would raise me above my failings.

God is love.

Beneath the rage was the pain. Beneath the pain was humility and acknowledgment of my personal depravity and poverty of spirit and beneath that there was God.

God is love.

It is not that God acts in love, though of course He does. It isn't just that He *does* love. It is that by His nature at the core of His being:

God is love.

Even if I deny Him by my betrayal of His blessings He cannot deny Himself.

God is love.

He cannot deny Himself and so He is always moving in love toward me. Love liberates, and so He shook what could be shaken, He took what could be taken, and He burned what could be burned. He left me naked in rage, in pain, and finally in humility. His love flowed within the depth of my soul as molten lava and I sensed in the deepest part of me something new.

I realized I was still lying on the ground. I was filthy. Perhaps I had never been so filthy in my life. What did it matter, anyway? I rolled over and looked up at the starry moonless sky. I felt something begin to rumble. Was it an earthquake? No, it was something coming from inside me.

Remarkably, I began to feel laughter rumbling out of me, until I was shaking with joy and life. I pointed up to the sky and shouted "YOU!" for I had felt God's embrace and now I felt His hope welling up within me. He had liberated me from my rage. He had liberated me from my pain and my fears. He had wept with me, and now He laughed with me, and with that laughter came the courage to hope. I was not dwelling on what was in the past nor contemplating the future, I was reveling in this moment of betrothal to Him. "I am His and He is mine and His banner over me is love" (see Song of Songs 2:16).

I lay there and I looked up at the stars as if to see His

face. Then I noticed something unusual in the sky. Way off on the horizon, I saw a really bright star, brighter than any I had ever seen before. I thought it might be a satellite. Then I remembered reading about the discovery of a new comet. It was Hale-Bopp coming to greet my new birth.

Every night for months as I walked, the new star journeyed with me. Always it reminded me of the work that God had done in me that night to set me on a new course with a new joy, the joy that comes only when you have been to hell and back.

The next day, the judge asked the children what they wanted. They said they wanted to spend equal time with both of us. The judge told Sue he would give her half custody if she agreed to return to California, and she did. He told me I could receive half custody, but only if I promised to learn to cook. I made that promise with all sincerity, but in truth all I was ever able to cook was frozen pizza.

On the twentieth anniversary of our marriage the judge signed the final divorce decree and I got drunk for the second time in my life. I did not try to figure out what it all really meant but in my stupor I remembered that the very first moment I saw Sue, I asked myself could I still be married to her in twenty years. I had answered myself yes, and to the day I had kept that promise. A year later, I went through the healing process and received an annulment through the Catholic Church.

The kids were back in school. It was in the early fall, the time of the hot Santa Ana winds that blow offshore. It was the time of brush fires in the canyon, so as I drove to County Line to escape for a surf, I took no note of the smoke haze drifting beyond Boney Ridge.

I got to the beach and paddled out. There were no young surf gromms in the water; they were with their soccer moms at soccer. The few of us in the water enjoyed the reverie of sharing uncrowded waves. The smoke came a bit closer, but we did not worry about it. We knew that these fires sometimes flew down the canyons with nothing to stop them until they hit the sea. But we did not know that these flames were coming straight toward us.

The smoke cloud loomed higher and higher and then the Santa Anas blew them directly toward County Line at menacing speed. Suddenly we realized that we were trapped. There was no sense going to our cars to drive away, and we would have to let them burn if that was to be their fate. I took off my rash guard and dipped it in the water and held it to my mouth, breathing through it as my eyes watered.

In spite of the sketchiness of the situation, when a good wave came we still paddled for it and rode it, except that we pulled out a little early. A good two hours passed as we waited out the firestorm. The sun above me had a strange orange hue. I found myself contemplating the last two years.

God had promised me that "everything that could be

shaken would be shaken, everything that could be taken would be taken, and everything that could be burned would be burned." I contemplated all that I had lost and all that had gone up in smoke. First my wife, and then my children. Fawn was following the Jack Kerouac road, Jeremiah distanced himself by spending most of his time surfing, and I had only half custody of my two youngest. My best friend turned his back on me when I told him I was getting a divorce, and even my dog, which Sue had taken to New Mexico, had been given away.

My rental house had been lost, then my cabin, and finally my home and all my possessions that it held. I had even put about a dozen surfboards out on the curb and put the local grommets on notice to come to pick out a board for free. The cars that had been paid for were borrowed against, and my investments were liquidated, and my bank account was underwater. I had lost everything, but I found great freedom in becoming a minimalist. I had lost all my hopes and dreams. I was thankful and amazed that I still had my business. I did not know that God intended to liberate me from that too.

All I had left were the clothes in my backpack, two surfboards, and some trophies. Now here I sat on my board covered, like my life, in ashes. The great shaking had liberated me and taken me down to the essential and that was simply the love of God.

Finally, it was safe to return to my car. I brushed the ash off the back window and put on the wipers so I could see well enough to drive. I did a U-turn and headed back along PCH to Thousand Oaks. I drove past blackened, burned-out underbrush. The thought came to mind that if I had lost a special gem in those mountains, the easiest way to find it would be to burn everything to the ground. I imagined finding a beautiful red jewel glowing in the sunlight upon the black, torched ground.

God had burned away all the weeds and revealed to me that in the midst of those ashes I was a beautiful red ruby glowing with the very redness of His redemptive blood. But a ruby has no brilliance or beauty to it except the beauty it reflects when the light shines upon it. I was revealed to be beautiful because His love shone upon me. Everything around me that could be burned could burn, for I had come to realize that God loved me more than I ever knew.

The swell window began to open less from the north and more to the west. The time of the winter swells were over and gone. Just as certainly came the spring.

CHAPTER 9

The Spring Swells

TANDEM SURFING, 1996–2000

It was the time of the spring swells, swells of new beginnings. I had exploded back to life, filled with a new kind of power, a new kind of resilience, determination, and joy. I felt an explosion of passion and hope and was just in awe at the delights of life itself. I began to explore new adventures, and even ventured into new discoveries within my soul.

I had rediscovered my own God-given identity. Until now, I had not realized the extent to which I'd sublimated my own desires, tastes, and ways to accommodate my ex-wife. It wasn't that she demanded this of me; I'd just been so determined to please her that I had forgotten what I wanted. I had lost touch with my own heart.

Now I learned that I did not like the walls painted beige, and that I preferred to eat dinner at five thirty rather than six thirty. I slept with my feet where my pillows belonged, and I lay diagonally across the entire king-size bed. I realize how trivial this sounds, but in a deeper part of my soul, I was also learning again to seek out the true desires that God had planted there. I had thrown everything up in the air, and I was discovering a whole new freedom, a whole new way of living, and a whole new way of relating to my interior self and even to God.

My entire identity had been wrapped up in being a husband, a businessman, a provider, and a father. Now, suddenly, I was single. My two oldest children were out of the nest, Fawn on her travels and Jeremiah on the flight deck of an aircraft carrier fighting in the war in Afghanistan. Though my two youngest preferred to live with me most of the time, I was free to leave for the day, the weekend, or even a week because Sue was always glad to have the kids stay with her. So within the context of taking care of my responsibilities as a father, I had maximum freedom to do and be whatever I desired.

But who was I?

Though I added sailing and long-distance paddling to my water time, my main passion of course remained surfing. I began to travel in search of perfect surf from deep down in Mexico as far south as the unknown little fishing village of Punta Mita (it's a fancy resort now), which was at the end of the road near Puerto Vallarta. It was so isolated that I surfed by myself naked. I sojourned as far north as my hometown of Santa Cruz, California, which was so cold that instead of surfing as nature intended I had to wear extra four-millimeter-thick wetsuits. My wanderlust resulted in my increasing the number of surfaris I took to Hawaii from just once a year to every few months. The fact that my parents lived there now certainly made it easier.

I was competing regularly as a member of the Malibu Surfing Association. We surfed club contests at gatherings of the tribe and various classic surf spots up and down the coast.

I was a good surfer, but I was not in the league of some of the incredible, smaller-framed surfers who would stylishly cross-step to the nose and hang ten like a hood ornament before cross-stepping back and doing a drop-knee turn. My son Jeremiah was one of the best surfers in the world. He would hang ten, and then casually dip his hand in the wave face to make his tail fin break loose, and he would helicopter it around 360 degrees and then accelerate down the line and bottom-turn to hit the lip way past vertical, twisting the nose as it arced above the wave back toward the peak, and execute a totally different kind of helicopter. He also loved to go big. He won contest after contest, and he would joke with me, "I guess surfing genes skip a generation, Dad."

"Yeah," I would respond, "but so do the genes for being bald—and I am not bald."

I found myself enjoying judging contests, not just for the free coffee and doughnuts they gave us, but for the camaraderie, and the talk story times between waves. I would climb the judges' tower in the predawn moments before a contest. It was usually cold and windy in the morning, so I would wear my blue Malibu Surfing Association jacket, blue jeans, and my Australian lamb's wool Ugg boots to stave off the cold until the sun burned away the morning fog. I was happy.

My good friend, the late, great, six-foot-two Michael Spence, would always bring me a big cup of coffee from his camper because he knew I was helpless when it came to the domestic skills required to make coffee. He was one of the "rockers," meaning he was one of the top longboard judges on the coast. Besides surfing, he was a rodeo cowboy, and he coached swimming and judged springboard diving. He was bigger than life, with long white hair and beard, and a huge belly. In time, he became known as the "Surfing Santa." Little did I know as I sat in the tower one early morning what a pivotal role he would play in my life as I developed a new world surfing tour.

Around eleven in the morning, I saw a massive surfer walking down to the beach, carrying an even more massive surfboard. I had never seen a board that big, but the next wave came, and I had to get back to judging. Then, ten minutes later, someone else carried a big board down to the beach and plopped it down next to the first one.

I looked over at Big Mike. "Dude, those boards are huge. They must be tandem boards. Is there going to be a tandem contest?"

He nodded under the straw hat that all judges and lifeguards seemed to wear. "Yeah. With the rebirth of cool, with longboarding becoming popular again, they have started to tandem again. That's Steve and Barrie Boehne down there. World champions back in the day. They were the only ones that kept tandem surfing alive for years here in Cali."

Three more big boards came down to the beach, and I watched the lithe women of tandem begin to stretch as the men postured in their alpha-male stances. I probably did a terrible job of judging the regular heat that was still out in the water because, when they began practicing beach lifts, I became transfixed.

"Mike, how do we judge it?"

He shrugged. "I don't know. I have never even seen a tandem contest before. They just told me if the lift looks hard and they surf pretty good while they are in a lift, throw them a high score."

The tandem teams paddled out, and I could not believe what I was watching. I had seen tandem as a child, but the only thing I remembered were women standing on men's shoulders while they surfed Steamers Lane in Santa Cruz. What I saw in the water now was much more extreme. It was the most beautiful expression of surfing I'd ever beheld. The teams would paddle in powerful, synchronized strokes with the man behind the woman, and then they would both get up as one as they dropped in and did a long, drawn-out bottom turn. Then, suddenly, the woman would leap as the man lifted her, and she would go into beautiful, graceful, long, arcing, and dangerous lifts.

The crowd was stunned. The whole beach froze and with every lift they screamed their amazement. The too-cool-for-school surfers on the beach were stoked like young grommets again. You could see the outright joy expressed by the tandem women while the tandem men scowled with the determined look of weight lifters. The men had to somehow lock in their core and their upper body while their legs remained fluid enough to surf and maneuver their boards.

I was blown away. How was this even possible?

The lack of organization and judging criteria extended to the water when one team dropped in on another. Dropping in or snaking someone like this is not allowed in regular surfing contests, but the contest director had said it would be okay for tandem, which seemed crazy to me, because it made this very dangerous sport of surfing even more dangerous.

As the teams came out of the water, the fiery Brazilian

wife of a member of one of the teams took a swing at the man on the team that had dropped in on them. Mike looked over at me with a twinkle in his eye and coined the phrase "tandem drama."

"Man and woman on a surfboard together," he said. "What else can you expect?"

I jumped up after the heat, waving for a replacement, saying I had to go to the bathroom. Instead, though, I caught up with the tandem teams. "What you're doing is incredible. How can I get started?" I asked.

With one voice, they replied, "Call Steve and Barrie Boehne."

As it turned out, the Boehnes had already left the beach, but I called them the next morning. Steve told me that he had just shaped a tandem board that would probably work great with my weight.

"Do you have a partner?" he asked.

"I'm working on it," I answered, though I had just begun to do so in that moment.

That night I went to the dojo where I taught, thinking perhaps one of the athletic women there would be interested in a new challenge. I was right. She was just over 120 pounds. She was a former champion figure skater and she was very close to getting her black belt. That meant she was athletic, flexible, and had a good sense of balance. The best thing was that she didn't surf, so we wouldn't have to worry about muscle memory as she learned to flow with me on the board. Our ninja fighting style often used the opponent's energy to defeat him, and this training would certainly help her tune in to my energy and to what I was doing.

We headed down to San Clemente a few days later and Steve and Barrie delivered my first tandem board to me. It looked like a big twelve-and-a-half-foot yellow banana slug, so that was what we named it. The Boehnes gave us our first tandem lesson down at Old Man's surf spot at San Onofre beach. We paddled out, and to our amazement we were able to do a few lifts. We came in, rested, and then paddled out again.

That day, a partnership was forged that would take us around the world tandem surfing. We surfed events up and down the coast. Our home break, Malibu, had long peeling rights that made it ideal for surfing well and doing multiple lifts on the same wave. We surfed eighteen-foot faces of a southern hemi swell at Swami's, and fourteen-foot faces of a cold winter swell at C Street in Ventura. She was a courageous, amazing partner. After half a year, we made it to the podium for our first trophy at Steamers Lane in my hometown of Santa Cruz. We traveled the world, surfing in Hawaii, France, New Zealand, and even in Australia, and usually making it to the podium.

I was stoked out of my mind. I felt that this was what I was born to do, and that God had healed my back so that I could. What if you were supposed to be the greatest boxer of all time but never got in the ring and tried it out? What if you were supposed to be the greatest painter in the world but never picked up a brush? What if God had a beautiful plan for our lives and we had tuned Him out to such a great extent that we missed out on it? I was forty years old and just now had discovered the most exciting, thrilling, and challenging experience in my life.

We scheduled a training trip to Hawaii. We flew in late in the afternoon, unpacked our brand-new tandem board, and headed down to the inviting waters of Waikiki. We stopped by one of the ABC stores and bought warm water wax. Diamond Head shone with the early golden light of the approaching sunset. We were excited to be out of our wetsuits and away from the cold California surf. We had escaped to the warm, crystal blue waters of Hawaii.

How often we wonder why God does not answer our prayers when we ask Him for something and then realize in retrospect that He did answer the prayer, only the answer was, "No," or "Not yet," or "Not here," or "Not with that person." Ultimately, we learn the value in patiently waiting for God to send just the right wave at just the right time. Patience really is just another expression of hope and faith in His love, His will, and His provision.

We set our board down next to the Duke statue welcoming us to Waikiki. We took our leis that we had received at the airport and draped them over his outstretched arms. I still follow this custom whenever I return from a trip. Little did I know that in the not-too-distant future I would own a condo on the beach just a couple of blocks away. Little did I know that the beach boy Smokey Bear Okuma, who approached us and showed us a new lift, would be someone I would one day install into the Tandem Surfing Hall of Fame that I would create. Little did I know that within a decade I would be hosting thirty-two teams for world championships at the very spot we were paddling out to surf and even win multiple masters world titles.

This is the way of it, isn't it? We have no idea of the intricate tapestry of our lives. It is only with hindsight that we can look back and see how God has guided our lives. "If you seek me with all of your heart I will let you find me. I know what I have in store for you; plans for peace, not destruction; a future reserved for you full of hope. If you seek me I will let you find me" (see Jeremiah 29:11).

Now here I was about to express this beautiful art form in the most beautiful place on a beautiful wave with a beautiful person. Some works of art, like paintings, sculptures, or even the beauty of the universe are made to last, suspended in time and space for us to enjoy. However, there is transitory dynamic art that expresses itself for only a matter of moments in time and then is gone: dance, or music, an infant's smile. Such is the beauty of the art of tandem surfing. I was the artist sweeping broad brushstrokes but I also had become the painting.

I knew how special this was. When my partner and I were doing a lift, we were probably the only people in the world doing so at that moment. How often can we say that? But with God, His call to each of us is just for us, and responding to Him leads us into a singularly unique relationship.

I was about to paddle out into ecstasy. I tied my surf leash to the double plugs on the tail of the board. I had asked my shaper to add a second plug, so if one popped out in the heavier Hawaiian surf, the other would hopefully hold. Our board was shaped with a narrower tip and extra rocker in the nose to handle the more critical drops here in the islands.

I put the board in the water to keep it cool while I waxed its virgin surface. Andi stretched out the tightness in her muscles and joints from the long plane ride. I spent a good ten minutes waxing the surface of the board, flipping it over in the water to cool it down again, and then waxing it in long circular motions to give it the sticky bumps my feet would need to grip it while we surfed.

When I finished, I dove underwater just to feel the negative ions fully revive me. I waxed up my hands and my shoulders, so when I gripped Andi or she gripped me, she would not slip. As she finished her stretching by going into deep splits, I tossed the wax to her and she put wax on her ankles, thighs, hips, and hands so we would stick to each other during transitions.

She was athletic and beautiful, and I was jealous of her six-pack. I brought the board back up under a coconut tree and laid it facedown so the sun would not melt the wax. There was enough rocker in it so that as it lay there no sand would stick to the wax. We found an open spot in softer sand, and we began to practice our lifts. I had been going to Hawaii at least once a year since 1984, and I'd been able to have fun and maintain a low profile. Now that I'd come to tandem surf, everything was different.

People on the beach took out their cameras to take pictures, but they had no idea that this was just our warm-up and that afterward we would jump on our board and paddle out. As we walked to the water's edge, someone stopped us and said, "Excuse me, but are you guys going to do that on the surfboard?"

"Yes," she responded, "it's called tandem surfing."

We paddled in synchronized strokes out the eighth of a mile to the surf spot called "Pops." From there, we paddled out to the deep channel alongside Pops and watched a set roll through. After another full set, we paddled over and eased ourselves close to the other surfers, showing our respect and our patience by letting a few sets go by before we positioned our board to catch a wave. The waves were breaking in perfectly shaped, hollow, ten-foot faces. It was perfect for tandem. Waves this big gave us enough speed to stabilize the board while also not being so out-of-control big that we were limited to doing just the less extreme lifts. We had about twenty different lifts we enjoyed doing, but there were two lifts that came so naturally and were so incredibly beautiful that they became our go-to lifts.

We paddled back to our takeoff spot against the current to be ready as a perfect set began to show itself on an outer reef. I knew this spot about as well as any wave in the world, as I had been coming to the islands for years and this was my favorite when I came here. She was excited to drop into her first Hawaiian wave, but she felt a bit wary because she was not used to surfing coral reef breaks. We had surfed bigger waves, but none that had seemed so fast or so hollow to her. Coral reefs did this. Waves come out of deep water and suddenly hit the reef, trip up, and throw. She had been resting with her back against my chest. She saw a big wave hitting the outer reef and then back off, and she looked at me and smiled.

"We go," I said.

We turned the board toward the beach as she lay down in front of me, her legs wide so I could scoot up close. Then she wrapped her legs around me and grabbed my thighs with her toes so that we would be as one person and so our weight would be distributed in as short an area as possible on the board. We paddled for the wave with all of our might.

She knew to always paddle as hard as she could while I calibrated the power and speed of my paddle to time our entry into the wave face. The wave began to hollow beneath us. The nose of our board was battling the fifteen-mile-per-hour trade winds that were blowing up its face and giving it just a small bit of a choppy texture. These offshore breezes we were battling were our best friends, though, as they would blow up the face, holding it up and not letting it throw until it had reached its full zenith, maximum power, and hollowness.

I yelled, "Toes!" and she knew to dig harder into my thighs and pull me forward toward the nose of the board with her toes. At the same time, I dug in hard on one more powerful stroke and threw my ankles hard toward the nose of the board. That provided an extra surge and suddenly we were at the tipping point and the board started to slide away beneath us into the steepest wave face that we had ever surfed on together.

We were nearly free-falling down the face. I called out "Right rail," but I knew she had already anticipated that I needed her to put just a little bit more of her weight on the right side of the board so that as she got up she would not accidentally fight the direction I wanted to go, or worse yet accidentally turn the board back into the pit in the jaws of the wave.

She felt my hands rub her hips as I pushed down on the

board to leap to my feet, so a split second later she did too, and we came up and back on the board as one person. As I got up, I wrapped my arms around her waist and pulled her back toward me so hard that her legs flew off the board. I needed her back with me and I needed her there right now if we were going to make this bottom turn and not pearl (having the nose of the board submerge under water in front of us). She flowed with my energy, and rested her back against my right pec and her head against my right clavicle. Her knees were soft so she would not push me off the board, and her feet were only two inches apart.

She tuned in to my flow as I leaned hard into the wave, going right, and executing the bottom turn as she squatted down as low as she could, kicking her left leg out in front of her to relieve the downward thrust on her that our powerful turn caused. She was amazing. She had helped me so much with our turn that we nearly flew out the back of the wave. I leaned back hard to the left, trying to rocket back down the face toward the wave's vortex.

I yelled, "Knee!" and she knew to collapse her legs and pull us both forward to help us get back on the center of the board. As I came back past vertical I reweighted and leaned right again, back into the face of the wave. Then I righted the board and put it in trim as we fired down the line listening to our board chatter on the slight wind chop. An instant later, I called out, "Turn!" as I twisted her hips to rotate her to face me to prepare for the jump. She did a perfect ballerina spiral, staying tight next to me while still keeping a little softness to her knees so that she would not push me off the board. She grabbed both of my shoulders with her hands as I grabbed her hips in a C-grip right at the bikini line.

She sensed my energy and flowed with me. As I sank my legs, so did she, and then she rocketed up, jumping with all of her might while pushing down on my shoulders. After my elbows got past ninety degrees, my hands rotated on her hips so that I was not gripping her with just my fingers. Now I was under her hips with the entire palm of my hands and I powered her up as she went vertical way above my head.

As she reached her zenith, she released both her hands from my shoulders and thrust her left leg locked out toward my right chest as she extended her right leg back horizontal to the board. I released my left hand from her right hip as she rotated it to the sky, and quickly grabbed the bottom of her left foot that she had extended down by my chest. She leaned way forward, extending one hand out, essentially standing in my left hand. I held her hip as she leaned over it horizontally. She extended her other hand behind her and slightly up at an angle. Her powerful abs locked her into the lift just in time for me to do a cutback. The wave was about to empty into the deep channel, and I needed to get back to the hollowing part of the wave on the shallow reef.

As we entered back into the hollowing wave, I saw that

we could extend the ride if we made a fast run for about a hundred yards back across the reef the same direction we had just come. We locked in the arabesque. I took her left foot and pushed it to my left quickly, and it flipped her sideways. I flipped her leg and caught her in a cradle. As she fell from the sky, she wrapped both of her arms around my neck, keeping her center of gravity tight to me. I slid her back to the board, facing away from me. I held her left ankle as she went down to the board with her right foot and I held on to her waist with my right hand. She grabbed the wrist of my right hand and placed her left hand on top of my head. As I sank my legs to go immediately into the next lift, I slid the palm of my hand from her right hip to the small of her back.

She pressed on my head and jumped with her right leg first, and then, pressing her left leg into my hand as I held her ankle, she stepped straight up in the lift as I pressed her up with my right palm in the small of her back. She reached up for the sky with both hands going as high as she could, until right at the point of weightlessness, in a seamless flow, she fell back into the palm of my hand in a hard, graceful arc.

She looked backward upside down into the wave face, her hands down behind my back, her head almost touching my face. I held her left ankle out in front of me, and she piked her right knee. We surfed like that for half the length of the hollow section, and then I just let go of her left ankle. She

131

was in perfect balance, and I held her there with only one arm as she suspended in space. I felt so alive and I could feel her tummy rumble a bit as she laughed. She remembered that this was not a good idea, and she screamed out in joy that, like a *chia* in karate, served to tighten her abs and her whole body. I cut back down along the wave face again, continuing to hold her above me with one arm like a chandelier, but now I began to rotate her slowly 180 degrees. Now she was staring upside down in the direction we were surfing, with her cheek resting against my cheek.

I reached out and took her left hand with my left hand. Then she grabbed my forearm with her other hand, and she held herself in a handstand while I still supported her by the small of her back. Then I popped her a bit, reversed my grip as she arched just a little more, and then she let go of my forearm and spread her arms horizontally across my chest. She was suspended in an incredible lift. I was holding her only by pressing up with the heel of my palm against just one inch of the small of her back.

The wave was beginning to fade, so I said, "Down," and she quickly brought her hands together and she dove straight down headfirst toward the board. My left arm caught her, and as I did, she let her legs kick out and she landed on her feet and came up facing me.

She pivoted again away from me and stretched both arms horizontally from her to her side. As I slid my arms under her armpits, she kicked out her legs and lifted them at a right angle in front of her and I gently lowered her to the board. She grabbed the rails and quickly slid forward eighteen inches to give me room to sit down, which I did.

I had just gotten to ride a perfect wave, in the most perfect place in the world, on a perfect surfboard, with a perfect tandem partner. We surfed a half-dozen additional perfect waves as the sun set. We paddled in at twilight, as the flames of the tiki lights lit up the shoreline. Life was good.

It dawned on me then that the woman on a tandem surfboard is a perfect metaphor for a soul in love with God. The woman puts her trust in the man, yields to the man, and tunes in and responds to what he is doing. A soul in love with God wants to tune in to Him. We want to have a dynamic, responsive, fluid relationship with God, don't we?

I remember once paddling into a perfect wave at Pops with a tandem girl and she hesitated as we got up because it would have been the biggest wave she had ever ridden. The words of Jesus ran through my mind: "Oh you of little faith, how much longer must I suffer you" (see Matthew 8:26). When we paddled for that wave I had already ridden it in my mind. But when the tandem girl hiccupped, hesitated, and threw off our timing, we lost the opportunity. I learned this and so many lessons from God, and nearly every day I paddle out I learn something new about my relationship with Him.

We want to paddle out with Him and wait on his wave

of the Spirit to come our way. At His leading, we want to turn and paddle into the next adventure with Him as our tandem partner. He is leading us in our lives. We want to paddle with all our might in hope and prayer and drop into a new, wonderful, rich experience of His perfect will. We want to flow with Him and rest in Him as He turns us in a new direction. Most of all, we want to take that leap of faith. We want to trust in Him and jump with all our might, knowing that He is there to catch us and lift us. We want to be led by Him to stretch out in new directions and follow our deepest God-given desires.

I had been crippled both physically by my back challenge and spiritually by the cares and worries of the world. I was born to be a tandem surfer. At the core of my being, I knew not only that God intended this, but that He took great delight in my expressing my innermost being and my physical ability.

But it was more than that. Even more certainly, I was meant to tandem surf with God. I realized almost from the beginning that my tandem surfing was meant to talk story to me about my own intimacy and responsiveness to God.

It was the time of the spring swells and I had come back to life. I was a tandem surfer and I tandem surfed with God.

CHAPTER 10

Dropping in Deep

THE TIME OF THE MOUNTAIN
SWELLS, 2001–2005

I paddled out into knee-high surf to ride the most enticing waves I had ever seen. I had just pedaled my bicycle across America from the Pacific Ocean to the Atlantic Ocean. It was the turn of the century, and it was my "Good-bye to the Mainland" tour. I was moving to Hawaii when I got back to Cali.

I had jumped on my bike at my son Jeremiah's navy ship, which was moored in San Diego. It took me all day just to get to the top of the steep coastal mountains. The next morning I headed down through eight days of record-breaking heat in the desert. It was so scorching that my bike tires dug grooves in the pavement. It got so hot that a quarter-inch of pavement clung to the tires. My only choice was to ride at night.

I climbed into the high desert, then over the Rockies, and then on across the heart of Texas for eight days. Halfway across, I found myself pedaling for a week into the teeth of the devastating Tropical Storm Allison. I finally made my longest one-day run of the ride on the last day into Jacksonville, Florida. Then I threw my bike on the rack of the truck that my daughter had been following me in, grabbed my board off the top, and now here I was, finally, surfing.

I paddled for my first wave and, as I stood up, I felt the numbing, gyroscopic effect in my equilibrium from pedaling the bike. At first my legs seemed wobbly, but then the surfboard knew what to do, and I rode the wave all the way to the shore. I paddled back out and sat on my board waiting for the next wave. My back was facing the late afternoon sun; the sun being in the "wrong" place gave me a twinge of adventure. As the small waves rose and fell beneath my board, I pondered my physical condition. The muscles on my forearms had Popeyed out and grown bigger. My leg muscles now often involuntarily twitched, as though lightning was randomly striking parts of my calves. Then there were the deep bruises that the handlebars had made at the bases of my thumbs on the palms of my hands. They ached a little, so I instinctively dipped them into the cool water. The deep blue bruises would continue to surface and grow darker for months to come, until finally disappearing more than a half year later.

I caught another wave and rode it close to where children were frolicking near shore. I kicked out, turned, and paddled back out, dipping my board and my head beneath the refreshing small breakers. The ocean had never felt so good.

I didn't feel tired at all as I sat on my board. In fact the feeling was quite the opposite. I had much more of a feeling of being cleaned and revitalized. It was as if every cell had the toxins flushed out by the flow of oxygen and nutrients that my blood had surged through me for the four weeks of my trip. I had drunk a great torrent of oxygen into my body and *ha* into my soul.

During those twenty-seven days of solitude on my bike, I had found myself slowly reliving the chronology of my life as well as contemplating my dreams. I found myself forgiving the failings and betrayals of others, and forgiving myself of my own failings. But one moonless night, I rode on in the kind of deep darkness you can find only in the desert. In that darkness, something broke free deep inside me. Something entirely unexpected happened. I heard the deepest part of my soul cry out, "I forgive You, God."

This seemed blasphemous. Who was I to forgive God? He had no need for my forgiveness for He is perfect love. Yet the secret reality that I had been hiding even from myself was that I was angry with God. How many times had He said no to my wants and needs—or worse yet just did not seem to care. This anger had to mean that I doubted

His goodness and I doubted His love's ability to comfort, provide for, guide, and protect me.

I thought then about how many times my not getting my way had turned out to be the best possible blessing. I could see God's protection and surprises as His love and wisdom guided me through the twists and unexpected turns that my life had taken. The painful events now seemed to make the most sense of all.

A flood of forgiveness from my inner soul flowed toward God. The full realization came to me that God, who lives in the eternal now beyond time and space, understood the linear time line of my life from beginning to end as a single *now* moment. He who knew me before I was planted in my mother's womb, He who is infinite in love and power, wanted more than anything for my joy to be complete, for He had created me to share in His own eternal felicity.

As I crossed the desert that night, I felt a deep upwelling within my soul. I heard myself cry out repeatedly, "I forgive You, God," and I had a deep sense of his response: "It's okay, son. It's not your fault. You did not know."

I felt that God had made me an *ali'i*, a ruler now of the sea, of my mind, will, and emotions. My soul had been filleted before God by God. I'd had my times of wrestling with Him and I had clung to Him until I came to an end of myself and He blessed me. The very finger of God touched the deepest part of my being and healed and strengthened me, and I felt my youthful vigor renewed as my will broke free with the power now to follow His will.

As I pondered these things, a good wave rolled in and I paddled for it. As I rode in, I saw my beautiful daughter, Fawn, who had driven the escort truck at a painfully slow speed across the entire country, waving me in. She could not stand it anymore—she needed to grab my board and paddle out herself. She had been a champion surfer in high school, and though she had moved to the desert of Santa Fe, she still loved the sea.

As I rode that last wave in, I felt the St. Christopher medal that hung around my neck fall off. I caught it just before it fell into the ocean. All surfers of my generation, regardless of their faith, wore St. Christopher medals. When we wanted to "go steady" with someone, we would give her our St. Christopher medal to wear. If a girl was wearing this medal, everyone knew she was dating a surfer. As Fawn came to grab the board, I asked her if she needed any quarters for the wave machine. She giggled, grabbed the board as if to say, "Get out of the way, old man," and paddled out. I put the necklace back around my neck, thinking nothing of it.

Two nights later, I paddled out again for a final surf before heading back. As I rode my last wave on the last day at sunset, I felt the St. Christopher medal fall off again. Once more, I was fortunate to catch it in my hand. I had worn this medal for years, and it had never fallen off. As I caught it, I continued to surf, then I raised the medal up to God, thanking Him for the journey across the United States and the journey my life had taken to this point. I asked Him to bless my new quests in Hawaii, and I let the medal fall from my hand into the Atlantic Ocean.

One week later, I found myself holding a one-way ticket as I flew to my new home in Hawaii. I realized that I had poured out my whole life as a libation unto the Lord. I had lost or let go of everyone, my business, and every possession. All I had with me was my backpack with a few pair of surf trunks, a few tank tops, a pair of flip-flops, and my laptop computer. My twelve-foot tandem surfboard and a big duffel bag full of my surf trophies and business awards lay in the cargo bay below me. When I arrived, my surfboard arrived with me, but my bag of trophies did not.

Let it go, let it go, let it all go, was all I thought.

My bank account held only the seed money I needed to start over. Everything that was of the mainland was no longer mine. Even my two youngest children had to be left behind, because at the last minute my ex decided they could not come. I was confident they would come live with me soon but at that point, God had kept His words to me that I had sensed a few years earlier. "Everything that could be shaken would be shaken and everything that could be taken would be taken and everything that could be burned would be burned."

I was forty-seven years old and starting over in every way. It was time to surf the new swells of Hawaii. I had nothing except my own savvy and a deep sense of being in God's will to propel me into my future. Each decision I made now would set trajectories in motion that would have long-lasting effects. It was a fresh start. I had a chance to press the reset button and direct my life's journey toward the true desires that God had placed in my heart.

It was a new millennium. It was the beginning of a new life. I was going home. Tears came to my eyes as Israel "IZ" Kamakawiwo'ole sang into my headset, *"Ua Mau Ke Ea O Ka Aina I Ka Pono"* ("the life of the land is perpetuated in righteousness"). This is the Hawaii state creed as first spoken by King Kamehamea III. I prayed that it would be so for me, for my children, and perhaps my children's children's children in this land. I was going home to Hawaii where the four elements are all so fresh and clean. We have the freshest air, the cleanest water, and even new fire and new earth from our volcano. I felt that newness in me. I breathed in the fresh air that the trade winds had mingled with the fragrance of flowers. I was ready to dive into Hawaii's pristine oceans, and I was ready for God to rekindle the fire within me and for Him to establish and make me *kama-aina* ("of the land"): a local.

I had rented a home on the base of Diamond Head right on the water, and by sunset my household was set up.

I had run out to buy a printer, a desk, a chair, and some office supplies. I was open for business. I grabbed my board for a quick twilight surf, and lifted my hands to God as I surfed the last wave in. I touched my new St. Christopher medal and thanked God for all He had done and all that lay ahead. I showered at the outdoor shower, toweled off, and walked into my new home. The trade winds blew the fragrance of the plumeria tree on the windward side of the house through my bedroom down the hall and into my office where I looked out the window. The fragrance of the flowers mingled with the unique volcanic fragrance of the crystal blue waters of the Pacific, which lay only fifteen feet in front of my desk.

Just outside my window, a local Hawaiian felt at ease bringing his child up to use my outdoor shower after a day at the beach. How wonderful the relaxed spirit of aloha is that so easily receives without presumption and embarrassment and gives with only gladness. As he left, they smiled and waved. He called out, "*Mahalo*, my braddah."

I threw him back the hang loose *shaka* hand signal. This was all I needed.

I sat at my desk looking past the monitor at the ocean. I was ready to roll. I had resolved to start my firm in an entirely new way. Instead of having a huge firm with lots of staff, office space, and overhead, as I had before, I would just have a simple office in my home. I would establish a boutique firm, being very selective about clients. I would focus on small dream-maker corporations and their owners, and I would orchestrate their entire financial life. I did not want staff beyond a personal assistant.

I loved my craft. I found no joy in overseeing other people doing it. I would not build a big business again. I was starting over with only sixteen clients instead of the six hundred I had left behind. I trusted that the firm would grow, but in a new way. I would take care of the needs of my children, but now I would do so with a more balanced life with plenty of time in my day to surf, to write, and to seek God.

I developed a pattern of rising around five a.m. My morning commute involved walking into the kitchen to pour a cup of Kona coffee and walking back to my office and clicking on the computer screen. I would take a breakfast break about sunrise to say aloha to God and to the ocean by walking out to the sea with my second cup of coffee. I would walk along the sand to the edge of a seawall with my peanut butter and jelly on a toasted English muffin. I found over time that the same beautiful *humu humu nuku nuku apu'a'a* ("trigger fish") would visit me every morning. I would toss him a couple of crumbs from my breakfast, and we became friends.

I was *pau hana* ("finished with work") by two in the afternoon. I would paddle my one-man, twenty-foot-long, superlight, carbon fiber outrigger surf canoe the three miles into Waikiki to get my mail and do my banking. As I paddled that canoe, I could see fish fifty feet below me. When you see fish this clearly they remind you of birds for they too live in three-dimensional space and I felt at times as I glided with the swells that I was flying too. I stored a surfboard in Waikiki, so I would paddle in and carry my canoe up above the high-tide mark on the sand, grab my board, and go out for a surf, often grabbing a girl with whom to go tandem surfing. I would paddle back home against the wind that wrapped around Diamond Head about sunset and then sit on my lanai and play my ukulele to the stars as they blinked on. Life had become much simpler.

Several months later, my life felt more in balance than ever. It was November, and the sun was rising late in the morning now, about six thirty. I had been up working for a couple of hours, and as I made a second pot of coffee, I noticed the bruises in the palms of my hands from my bike ride were barely visible anymore. I had a short action list that day, and I felt a sense of relaxation come over me. The south shore surf was flat to ankle high. Maybe I would take the rest of the day off and just drift along and surf through the day; read the whole paper, play my ukulele, do some surfboard repair, and just go for a paddle in my outrigger.

I walked to the shore to have my toast and coffee with my friend, the trigger fish. The myna birds had begun their morning chorus to the Hawaiian steel guitar that played gently from my window. This was the kind of day travel posters are made of.

I felt a vibration in my pocket telling me a call was coming in. Should I ignore it? Life was bliss right now. Why answer it? Even as I decided not to answer it, though, my hand involuntarily reached into my pocket.

"Whassup?"

"Surfs up! Waimea's breaking. It's the first winter swell on the north shore. Get your heavy water leash and bring da *kine* for me! I can't find my wax."

Hmmm, I thought, *he needs wax*. The month before, this "friend" had offered to wax up my board and used a bar of soap instead. When I put my board in the water, my new tandem partner jumped on and slipped right off the other side as soapy bubbles filled the ocean around us. It took an hour to scrape off the soap and then rub the board with sand to remove the residue. Then I had to rub on a whole new base coat of sticky wax on the board surface.

Waimea was breaking. Was I mentally and physically ready for it? I felt in better shape than I had ever been in my life, and I would need to be if I was to paddle out in this huge surf. These would be the biggest waves I had ever seen, let alone ridden. I had made some big drops for sure, but nothing bigger than eighteen-foot faces. Eighteen feet was like an invisible concrete barrier in my mind. It was a wall to me, just like the four-minute mile was for runners, or the sound barrier was for pilots.

In my yard was the twelve-foot Brewer big wave elephant gun with a pin tail, single glassed-in fin, and narrow tip that rose abruptly at the nose to keep it from pearling under water as I dropped into a steep wave. Brewer custom-shaped this board for only one wave—Waimea. The board had rested, idling like a dragster at the starting line, all summer long. I had the right equipment but did I have the right stuff? Did I have the guts to paddle into a giant mountain?

The reef at Waimea is so deep that waves don't even begin to break there unless the faces are more than twenty feet. Waimea breaks less than thirty days a year. When the other big-wave spots on the north shore are closed out into one big, unridable wall, that is when the waves just begin to show themselves on the deeper reefs of Waimea. It only breaks when the waves are, as the Hawaiians say, *hehe nalu*, or "mountain waves." Memories of watching film of Waimea as a small boy brought to mind images of big wipeouts, long hold-downs, and near-death experiences.

As a waterman, I had always wanted the ultimate rush of surfing this ultimate wave. I had sustained my cardio since my bike ride six months earlier by hiking trails along the volcanic ridges near my home with twelve-hundred-foot elevation gains that were so steep at times I needed ropes to finish the climb. I was as fit as I probably ever had been or would be. It was a now-or-never moment, and I felt compelled to go for it.

David Pu'u, the great surf photographer and dear friend, beeped the horn of an old aqua-blue-and-white '64 Ford Fairlane. I threw my board on top of the two other boards on the beat-up old surf rack. There was someone else with David, and he had never surfed Waimea either. He seemed casually stoked. He grabbed my ukulele and started strumming the only song he knew. "Everybody let's surf a oo owah oo oo wah oo surf." At least the words were easy to remember.

David was an expert waterman—a former professional surfer, as well as a powerful swimmer with his short fins on. It was a privilege to me that he called me his friend. He knew I felt I was literally in over my head, but he had confidence in me and that filled me with a certain wary kind of boldness.

I had my full-on, stoked-to-da-max adrenaline surging through my veins. My guts were squirming more than the time I had sat in a plane as it slowly circled and ascended to 12,500 feet for my first jump.

As we drove down the hill from the sugarcane fields, we could see massive surf running along the entire north shore. The huge waves created a misty kind of fog by breaking and throwing up frothing steam that blew three miles inland toward us. Why had I answered the phone? I'd gone from the most peaceful, carefree morning to the highest octane day of my life. I had emotional whiplash.

We pulled into the parking lot, and Pu'u busied himself with his camera as I leashed and waxed up. There was nothing left to do but to walk as casually as I could manage toward the right side of the bay. There was really only one place to paddle out and only one way to get back in. Anyone who tried to take a shortcut would find themselves pounded into the sand by the huge shore break.

Wannabes paddle out having no sense of the danger they are in. They want to say they have surfed the bay, even though they have no intention of catching a wave. Just a few days later, a poser paddled out like this and when he got close to the impact zone, he freaked out. Sometimes when a riptide carries people out they think, *Wow. This isn't bad at all. I'm really strong today.* As the current carries them along, they falsely assume they can swim or paddle back in as easily as they got out. They don't realize they are riding a current that is a one-way freight train.

This surfer showed his lack of big-wave knowledge by not knowing that the only way he could get in safely was to paddle into the impact zone and catch a big wave after it had broken or catch a smaller fifteen-foot wave at the inside break called "Pinballs." To get in, a surfer needs to hug the right side of the bay and stay in the river of water flowing toward the shore. If they drift into the riptide going back out and to the left, the current will pull them toward the left of the bay and resist their efforts to paddle in.

Instead of doing this, the surfer shied away from the apparent danger of the breaking waves and paddled into the calmer waters of the current that would eventually gently sweep him to his destruction. This is the way in life, isn't it? When we try to take shortcuts that lack integrity, we often end up putting ourselves and others in dire circumstances. When we choose the harder but right way, we ultimately end up better off.

The poser drifted toward the left of the bay and found himself paddling very hard but not getting any closer than a hundred yards from shore. The lifeguards screamed through their megaphones at him to paddle back out to the lineup a half mile away and make another run for it. A huge set rolled under him and exploded between him and the shore. He had just dodged getting pounded. He would not be so lucky with the next set that came up quickly on him.

The first two waves passed under him, but a third, bigger wave exploded on top of him. We wondered how he could possibly survive that. After about ten seconds, two pieces of his board popped up. Fifteen seconds later, he popped up right next to the back of his board. He swam to it and grabbed it. This was a bad idea. His only hope for safety was to dive deep and hope the power of the wave passed over him. Instead, he clung to the board as the next wave drilled him. The wave rolled up on shore depositing both pieces of his board. He was nowhere to be seen.

Moments passed into minutes and his body never popped up. During a lull, the lifeguards went out on Jet Skis looking for him in the boiling water. Finally, about ten minutes later, a wave threw him on the beach about two hundred yards down current from where the pieces of his board came in. He lay facedown in the sand while the lifeguards ran up the beach. Just as they arrived, he shook his head and then pulled himself to a crawling position. He was very lucky to be alive.

As I waded across the small stream that flowed from the waterfall three miles inland from the valley above, I looked up at the cross that towered over the Catholic church on the hill above Waimea, and then scanned the cliffs even higher, knowing that there was an ancient rock altar (*heiau*) where the early Hawaiians had worshipped. Waimea made you stop and consider the fearful power of the one who sent the waves and to ask for His protection. I remembered my new St. Christopher medal. I touched it and prayed for God's *manna* and *manao*. Waimea was the winter home of the *ali'i*, the kings of Hawaii. No *kanaka* ("commoner") had been allowed to surf there in ancient days. Today, I was only a *kanaka*. However, if I successfully surfed here, perhaps, I would be *ali'i*.

I stood in the deep sand of the steep shoreline and watched for a half hour, timing the lull between sets and seeing where the edge of the lineup was and where the deep channel began at the edge of the shallow reef that caused the waves to trip up and break. I was trying to determine my lineups with markers on the land that would let me know where the safety zone of the deep channel would be. I counted how many waves there were in a set. Wave knowledge is critical, but my nerves were starting to boil over. I needed to get off the beach and paddle out or I never would.

Though they were breaking nearly a half mile offshore, the waves still looked huge as they broke in long slow arcs. You can judge the size of distant surf by how long it takes the lip to throw and then hit the bottom of the wave. These waves looked like they were breaking in super slow-mo. I realized that if I wiped out I would be held under for a long time before I came up again, and then I would have to grab a big gulp of air before the next wave dumped on me and held me under again. No help would be able to get to me for a while.

As the waves loomed on the horizon, the lifeguards began to call through their megaphones, "Everyone get back from the shoreline. A big set is coming!" I waited on the top of the sandy slope and let that set of waves roll up over my legs and surge around me. I hoped Waimea was peaking and that it would not get any bigger. I waited for the last wave of the set to roll through the shore break, and as it receded back out to sea, I grabbed my ankle leash and ran as hard I could, launching my board on the back of the rip wave going back out to sea. I paddled as hard as I could to stay with it and use its powerful current to help pull me past the shore pound.

I paddled at full throttle, hoping to make it out past the three hundred yards of shore break before a sneaker set came through. I paddled through swirling, boiling, and frothing rip currents and felt the push and pull of water upwelling and then sucking my board and me down all at the same time. I was committed now. There was no turning back. I had to get through this zone as fast as I could.

I was suddenly beyond the shore break and into the deep channel. I hugged the reef as close as I could without being in the impact zone and easily paddled out, letting the powerful riptide sweep me out toward the lineup like a Hawaiian ski lift to the surf zone. These strong currents are like my big Samoan friends. If you understand and respect them, they can be your best buddies. If not they can be your worst nightmare.

I made it to the edge of the impact zone and sat safely in the deep channel catching my breath and looking sideways into the lineup at the dozen or so brave souls waiting for the set. I saw a building set out on the horizon as they all suddenly began to paddle a little bit deeper and farther out. I eased my way a little deeper into the safety of the deep channel and watched with awestruck fear as surfers drew their lines and paddled into death-bomb waves and surfed horizontally along the wave face to the safety of the channel where I was. I heard the waves explode with the sound of thunder. I looked down at my board and saw the beads of water on it quiver as the waves' impact sent shock waves through the water to me.

This was my first Crazy Todd sighting. I saw someone paddle as if to catch a huge wave and then at the last second just purposely launch himself in a swan dive into the pit. It was the craziest thing I had ever seen. I found out later that he does that on the first wave of every new winter season as an offering of himself to the ocean, a humbling acknowledgment of its power and to "just get over the first wipeout, dude."

As the last wave of a set passed by, I paddled out to the takeoff zone. With waves like this, there can be no false bravado, just like the first time you skydive. When you skydive you have to hold the tentacles of your emotions together for only fifteen minutes, from taking off from the runway to jumping out of the plane. Surfing Waimea was like living in suspended animation for an eternity in a land of giants, hoping no one steps on you.

I sat in the takeoff zone letting two more sets roll through, determining the trajectory of my drop and what my line-ups were on the land so I would be in the right takeoff spot because we tended to drift a bit with the current during the lull between sets. I was ready, but Pu'u could tell I needed a little nudge to get me past the tipping point. He had been waiting in the channel with his camera. Now he swam into the impact zone in front of me. As a smaller fifteen-foot wave passed under me without breaking, he yelled up to me from below, "My grandmother wearing army boots can ride waves bigger than this!"

That broke my trance and, as the next set rolled in, I waited for the last and biggest wave of the set and paddled for it. I didn't necessarily want the biggest wave of the set, but I definitely wanted the last one. If I wiped out I did not want to be tumbled by ten more waves breaking on my head.

I paddled with all my strength down the face of the largest wave I had ever seen. I reached far and stroked deeply into the wave as the mountain of water sucked me higher and higher. The surging water upwelling from the reef below boiled as I paddled through it, and I could feel it pull my board right and then left and then release me as I stared into the pit. It was too late to pull out. I was committed, whether I wanted to be or not. Every sinew in my body and every fiber of my soul powered into that wave. There was a sense of the awesomeness, of the purest, cleanest fear, but more than that at the very core there was a peaceful feeling that I was in God's hands.

Suddenly a memory came to me of my father perching me up on the edge of our garage roof when I was about five and extending his arms, telling me to jump. I was frightened, but I felt safe as I leaped into his arms. Now, I felt that I would be leaping into God's hands. I felt His fearful, powerful love as I fell off the cornice, down the blue concave face, sliding down into the pit.

I had wanted this moment since I was a child. My soul screamed, *Go for it!*

I had no worries or cares on my mind. I was only focused on this moment. I felt that feeling of being at the still point, of stepping off a precipice into the eternal now. If I did not make the drop and the critical bottom turn, the breath I was gulping in would be my last.

Death was knocking. I felt totally alive.

As time stood still, I felt every vibration and nuance to the balance of the board, and I clung to the rails an extra moment as the fast-twitch muscles throughout my body tuned in to the feel of the board. As I stood up, I saw a rib running in the wave as it formed into a mogul. This could get ugly fast. I bent my knees to set my center of gravity lower, and prepared to use the flex in my legs as shock absorbers, so as I surfed over the speed bump I would not go airborne.

As I hit it, the board broke free momentarily, but the mass of my board held its line and stabilized as the fin grabbed deeper. The wave face was the most beautiful, most powerful, most fearful place I had ever been in my life. Was this a taste of what it would be like to see God? I felt Him smiling at me, because I know He takes pleasure in our stepping out of our comfort zones because this takes faith, and He is a big fan of faith.

The drop on a wave like this is similar to the one-minute free fall when you skydive and you hope the canopy will open when you pull the rip cord. Would I make the bottom turn? I had only once chance; there were no mulligans in heavy surf. Would I set my trajectory right so that the jaws of this powerful wave would not swallow me up and have me for lunch? I started to ease into the bottom turn so I could surf to the right along the face of the wave. The board was so big and going so fast that it did not respond, so I reached out and dragged my hand in the wave face and pressed down hard with my back leg on the board. The board responded like a cutting horse and redirected me from going straight down to drawing a line along the wave face.

I was nearly weightless as I free-fell down the face, but then I pulled powerful g-forces as I bottom-turned. I went back up the face diagonally, and I momentarily went weightless again and then leaned left on the downward rail a bit and was able to set the trajectory to fire straight across the wave face toward the channel. I flew by Pu'u as he reeled off pictures, and I knew if I could just hold this line, I would be in the safety of the channel in fifteen seconds.

Then suddenly I was in the peaceful tranquillity of the channel. I felt that I could do anything. I was alive with the power that God shared with me through that wave.

I paddled back out to the lineup, and as I sat in the take-off zone, I realized two things. First, that my pointer finger was pointing in the wrong direction. I must have dislocated it when I buried my hand in the wave face to make the bottom turn. I tugged on it a bit until it finally started to behave itself and point in the right direction again. Then I absent-mindedly reached up to adjust my St. Christopher necklace and I noticed that it was gone. It was somewhere beneath me in the very depths, in the very heart of sacred Waimea.

I realized that I had come full circle since that night in Jacksonville when I let another St. Christopher medal fall into the Atlantic. I had gone forth and now I was home. I had ridden over giant mountains on my bike in the mainland, and now I had ridden giant *hehe nalu* mountain waves in my new home. *There will always be mountains*, I thought, *there will always be giants*. It is there that we get to experience God the most, when He is right along with us providing His power, grace, wisdom, guidance, and protection. It might be huge, for the wildness of God is powerful and beyond our control. But He wants us to fully commit, to "go for it," as

Crazy Todd often screams at me. "Don't back down." Of course, this is usually when the waves are only ankle high. But the point is in big or small surf we always have fun and so it is with the Lord. We were created to enjoy that ride.

God uses the challenges that we overcome, as well as the challenges that result in a wipeout in our lives to infuse His humility into our souls and then impart a sense of an overcoming strength and peace so that we can tandem surf with Him. There is a peace that comes from things being in order. There is a peace that comes after winning a great war. Then there is "the peace of God that passes all understanding" (see Phillipians 4:7), and that is simply the bliss of the presence of God. We just need to lean into Him as I leaned into that wave face to make my turn.

To really live life, we must take risks. Taking risks takes faith. I am not speaking of foolish risks, because that is tempting God, and we should not put God to the test. I am talking about taking leaps of faith that bring us more deeply into the will and presence of God. We are not called to be average. We all have greatness within us, for we are made in God's image. We are called to greatness. God may fill us, but He wants to give us a larger and larger capacity to be filled, and He uses challenges and obstacles in our life to stretch out our capacity. Why be a thimble filled with God's aloha, *manna*, and *manao* when we can be an ocean filled with His love, power, and wisdom? Our response to challenges and suffering is what expands us.

There really is no such thing as a great surfer; there are only great waves. Those great waves invite us to share their greatness when we ride them. Perhaps, if we are humble enough and brave enough, they will even impart their *manna* and *manao* to us. So it is that God sends us His waves. He wants us to paddle in with all our heart, ride them, and become one with them.

It was the time of the mountain swells, and God shared His *manna* with me.

I I

The Swells of Mastery

2006–2008

I drove back over the Pyrenees reversing the same ninety-minute course I had followed in the predawn hours from Biarritz, France, to Pamplona, Spain. I parked the little red Citroën in the true French style by jamming it halfway up the curb, literally between a rock and a hard place. I walked through the crisp morning air to get *un café* (yes, I speak food French) and *un pain au chocolate* (okay, I got two of them)—and, oh yes, my tandem partner, for a morning practice session. When I knocked on her door about ten thirty in the morning, she greeted me with a yawn and sleepy eyes. "I thought you were going to run with the bulls this morning."

"Well, yes. I did that in my spare time between four a.m. and now." That is what life can be like. While some are out living life to the fullest, others sleep through it all. "The tide is just about right. Let's get in a tandem session!"

Her eyes lit up as she lifted two fingers. *"Dos minutos, mon ami."*

"Don't mess with me; I know that's Portuguese."

We walked to the cliff edge and saw beautiful lines of waves peeling from the point to the right where the small castle stood guard over the Côtes des Basques. We briskly walked down the one hundred steps to the contest site below. There were forty or so vendor tents and one big one in the middle where competitors stored their boards under the watchful eye of Fat and his men. I had a feeling that if they had been a generation younger, they would have been part of the French Resistance.

A forty-foot-tall wood silhouette of the Duke stood at the top of the cliff. My boyhood hero and father of aloha, Duke Kahanamoku, had brought back tandem surfing about a hundred years earlier when he leaned down and lifted a young surfer to his shoulders.

Though the water temperature barely reached seventy degrees, the sun warmed us and we were glad we left our wetsuits behind. Surfers who sat on the wall looking twenty feet below them watched the surf and took no notice of the barely clothed women of France who lay here and there on the wall and on the sand below, but they jumped with excitement when they saw my tandem partner and me carry our big board down to the beach.

It was July, around Bastille Day, and thousands had come to watch the world longboard title, but even more had come to see our tandem surf contest. Expectant eyes watched us as they took note of my partner holding the nose of the huge board and me carrying the back behind her. We worked our way toward the surf several hundred feet away on the wet sand, which had been covered in two feet of water only an hour before. The tidal swings here were more dramatic than at any place I had ever been.

We laid down the board as the media and the spectators crowded around us. My partner stretched for a good fifteen minutes and I pretended to stretch as I observed the lines the surf was taking that day. Conditions were perfect and, with any luck, the afternoon onshore wind would hold off for another hour or so.

We had a great session tandem surfing below the cliffs in front of a small castle. Eventually, the extreme French tide forced us all back up on the sea wall. The session ended early, but it was cool because I had a meeting that would forever change the course of tandem, so we paddled into our last wave and my partner, Jacque, jumped into a perfect lift. The slowly shallowing water made it very difficult to judge the depth, so teams had trouble gauging when to dismount. If they dismounted early, they lost valuable time to do another lift. Far worse, if they came down late, the board would abruptly stop and the man would fall forward with the tandem girl flipping out of control. I had a secret way to deal with this. I took out the screw from the front of my tail fin so that when the fin hit the sand it would hinge backward, making it six inches shorter and allowing me to quickly catch my partner and walk off the board onto the sand. Don't tell anyone.

We walked up the cement pathway and paused to give autographs to our French fans. I had dreamed up the concept of hosting a world title in Hawaii three years ago and a friend of mine had a similar vision. We would gather the thinning ranks of the tandem diaspora to the birthplace of surfing, Oahu, which appropriately means "the gathering place."

There had been only one true world title championship held in the last thirty-five years, and that had been in Australia eight years before, in 1998. Tandem had experienced its renaissance, but now due to poor judging rules, poor judges, and the ensuing "tandem drama," the active world-class teams had dwindled to less than sixteen and there were only a handful of contests in the world.

I had helped teach him a few years earlier and had given him a quality tandem surfboard. Since it was so difficult to get big boards, wherever I traveled to tandem I would teach people and then give a quality tandem board to the person who seemed most likely to help me perpetuate the sport.

By the second cup of *café* we had formed the International Tandem Surfing Association. His job would be to pursue sanctioning by the International Surfing Association, which is the Olympic arm of surfing, and I would pursue the daunting challenge of getting a suitable high-profile venue in Hawaii and the $50,000 it would take to pull it off.

My friends Mike Spence and David Pu'u warned me that organizing surfers—especially tandem surfers—was worse than herding rabbits and asked me if I was really ready to have egos pressure me from all sides. "Remember those old cowboy movies, Bear?" Mike said. "You could always tell the pioneers by how many arrows they had in their backs."

"I feel God's blessing and I feel His presence," I responded. "I sense that I am in the middle of His perfect will and I will do this. Many Hawaiians have told me that they believe that God has brought me to the islands to help revive and perpetuate this ancient, beautiful art form. I will ride this wave. How can I lose? I am tandem surfing with God! Their physical threats and their assaults on my reputation only matter to me if they matter to God. If it's important to Him, He will take care of it. If it is not important to Him, I will learn about humility. God knows I need more of that."

And so we surfed through all the angst and jealousy and we established something incredible. It was worth it.

I was passionate about starting new teams. In the months leading to the world title, I had developed about sixteen new teams in Waikiki, which essentially doubled the number of quality tandem teams in the world. Some would go on to spend a huge amount of time on the podium and even win world titles. The challenge was that, for every hundred women who want to tandem there is only one male willing to try it, because they didn't want to look too weak or clumsy and lose their cool factor in the water. Among our top teams, though, are some of the very best watermen in the world.

Months went by and now the time for the First ITSA/ISA Duke's OceanFest world title was at hand. Every day I saw more teams on the beach and in the water. The tribe was coming! One or two teams at a time, like ninjas emerging from the shadows. Waikiki was about to experience the rebirth of tandem. Tandem was starting to dominate the lineups. I watched people on the beach and those in the water come alive with excitement.

"Did you see that?"

"What?"

"Out there, that guy on the surfboard just lifted a girl over his head with one hand."

I imagined them going back to Nebraska or Italy or wherever and nonchalantly saying, "Oh yes, it is very common in Waikiki to see two people on a surfboard doing lifts. Don't you know that is the way they all like to surf in Hawaii?" What had been an extremely rare sighting for a whole generation was commonplace for these two weeks. My dream had come true.

The night before the contest, the Moana Hotel rented huge floodlights and we surfed in front of a thousand amazed spectators. The next day, twenty-eight teams from around the world lined up in front of the judges' tower. The men stood with their surfboards arrayed upright behind them like warriors waiting to go into battle with their partners standing in front of them. I found champion tandem surfer Rabbit Kekai, who was now eighty-five years old. "Uncle Rabbit, you got to see this." I put my arm around his shoulder as we walked him around to the *makai* ("ocean") side of the tower. He saw the first couple of tandem boards and I could see he was thinking, *So what, I have seen tandem boards before.* Then, as we came around the corner and he saw the twenty-eight teams standing together, I saw his heart leap and a twinkle or perhaps a tear in his eye. "I have not seen this since Makaha forty years ago."

We brought him right into the middle of the group shot where he knelt next to me with my two Ambassadors of Aloha: the legendary "Gidget" (Kathy Kohner-Zuckerman, who gained fame through a number of films and a Sally

Field TV series) and my mate Andrew King of Australia, with his curled, old-school, British military–style mustache. Mike Spence and I knelt next to each other behind the koa wood board that my friend and big wave rider Professor Tom "Pohaku" Stone had fashioned the way they did before Captain Cook first found the islands.

After the shoot, we all paddled out together and formed a big circle beyond the surf spot called "Queens." Some photographers followed us in an outrigger canoe. I wanted David Pu'u to feel special, so I made sure that he did not get a ride and had to swim out with all his heavy camera equipment.

I asked Archie Kellepa, the head lifeguard of Maui, to make an opening statement. Archie was one of the innovators of tow-in surfing, and he'd once nearly killed me when I went out behind a Jet Ski with him in giant surf in Maui on the day before the first tow-in contest in history. He was both competing in the event and in charge of ocean safety. Archie spoke to us of the greatness of the Duke and how he knew Duke was watching us and how pleased he must be. He talked about how great the sport of tandem surfing is and those who participate in it are. Then each team introduced themselves, some even brought water from their oceans to mingle with ours and then, as is the custom, we all splashed water into the air in celebration as we rejoiced in the gathering of the tandem tribe.

What happened next was unplanned. We all paddled over to the Canoes surf spot to free surf in the golden light of the setting sun. We all just happened to line up about six feet apart from each other in a solid line across the outside of Canoes surf break. I was Diamond Head side of everyone so I yelled to pass it down the line to wait for my signal that we were all going to try to catch the same wave. The Duke must have been watching and God must have been listening, because He sent us a perfect set wave that walled up the width of the entire surf break.

I yelled out "Charge!" Twenty-eight teams paddled for this wave. Twenty teams caught it, and we all did lifts. We rode to the beach exuberantly laughing.

The next morning God sent us absolutely perfect surf. I gave the judges the heads-up before our four-team heat paddled out. I told them that my tandem partner Shannon and I were going to do something that I had never seen anybody but me do before, and I had pulled it off only once. I told the judges that we were going to ride the wave for nearly an eighth of a mile—twice as far as the other teams were able to go—and we were going to head toward Diamond Head all the way toward the jetty and then shoot the narrow five-foot gap. They had no idea what I was talking about. But I grabbed Mike Spence's arm.

"If we get a long ride don't look away. Expect the unexpected."

Mike looked at me. "You're crazy. You're gonna shoot that gap? I don't care if you kill yourself; it just means more waves for me. But take care of Shannon." Shannon was among the new tandem surfers I had taught that summer. She brought her New Jersey spunk and spontanaeity with her when she moved to the islands, and she was a blast to surf with.

Crazy Todd overheard us talking. "If you die, I get your board, right? Just don't hurt the board."

Most people don't even know this barely visible gap even exists, but I know about it because it is directly in front of my home. The judges could not even see the gap from their tower.

We won our first heat, so as we paddled out for our second heat, I said to Shannon, "The tide is right, the swell direction is right, the surf is big. We can make it down the line and nurse the wave to make the connection. Let's shoot the gap."

She smiled and said, "Let's go for it, Bearski!"

On our second wave, we executed a one-arm back, then a falcon, and then a reverse one-hand falcon and I brought her down to the board with her still standing. We continued, trying to connect to the inside reef as the wave temporarily backed off in deeper water. Shannon relaxed and flowed, responding to me as I nursed the board through the section where it tended to back off before it rebuilt again. Then the wave started to rebuild over the razor-sharp shallow reef, and as the wave built and our speed increased, so did the energy of thousands of spectators. We were totally focused, but we could hear them screaming.

They were amazed that we had made it twice as far as any team had that day. All the judges except Mike had stopped watching us until his voice boomed out as he looked through binoculars. "Yellow team still up!" The crowd screamed louder than I had ever heard before.

As we approached the rocky jetty, it looked to everyone like a dead-end wall. The crowds continued to scream in appreciation of our long ride, but then their shouts turned to screams of terror. "They're going to hit the wall! He's crazy! Oh my God!" The judges stood up in their tower leaning out and looking through binoculars.

The tide was just high enough to make it through the narrow, shallow gap. Just as we reached the narrow opening, I steadied the board and I raised Shannon into an overhead lift. The crowds got even more frantic with fear as they imagined the board crashing into the rocks and my partner and me draped over the jetty, dead. Then we shot the gap and everyone went wild. We went the remaining forty feet to the protected kiddie pool, and I flipped Shannon in a cradle in both my arms and stepped off the board onto the sand. We could hear that everyone was blown away.

Thinking back on this event, I realize that when we see

only dead ends in front of us, if we open to God, He will make a way. Just as there was only one narrow gap for my partner and me to surf through at the end of our ride, there is a narrow gap for us on our path to intimacy with God. For me, that gap is Jesus, for He said, "It is easier for a camel to pass through the eye of a needle then for someone to be saved, but with God all things are possible" (see Matthew 19:22). He said, "Wide is the path that leads to destruction but narrow is the gap and straight is the way that leads to life" (see Matthew 7:13). He said, "I am the way and the truth and the life. No one comes to the Father except through me" (John 14:6 NIV).

I had to thank God for His blessing me to get to live that moment. No one watching knew what He and I had been through together. I was living the verse, "I glory in my weakness, for when I am weak then I am strong" (see Corinthians 12:9). I could almost hear Him laughing with delight. He had taken the man with a horrible back problem, healed him, and enabled him to surf at a world-class level.

Shannon and I accomplished what we did because we were of one will. We were committed to taking the risk to trust in each other to each do what we did best and to believe that we could make it.

I did not know, however, that my most thrilling tandem ride was yet to come.

12

The Wave of Betrothal

2008–PRESENT

One late afternoon, as is my habit, I was training some of the new teams on the beach in front of Duke's Restaurant. I sensed that someone was watching me. I glanced out of the corner of my eye and saw this stunning woman with long dark hair and skin so tanned that it was the color of koa wood. *She must be wondering what this weird man is doing*, I thought. *Maybe he's the oldest cheerleader in the world.*

The next day, as I was returning from my daily beach walk, I saw her again. She stepped down to the shoreline as if to intercept me as I walked by. The most beautiful girl on the beach wanted to talk to me. She spoke to me with the sweetest voice and with a slight accent that I could not place.

"Excuse me, but I saw you lifting some girls yesterday. Can you tell me what that was all about?"

I started to move my lips, but her beautiful hazel-green eyes left me speechless. I willed myself to speak and to remember to breathe out. As casually as I could, I responded, "Oh, that is tandem surfing. You look like an athlete. Do you do any sports?"

"Well yes. I used to do gymnastics." She failed to tell me that she had been on eight national champion gymnastics teams in Sweden.

"You would be great for tandem. Do you want to try?"

"I don't know. I have never really surfed, so I don't think I could do it."

I still needed to remember to breathe. "Actually, it is easier if the girl does not know how to surf when she is first learning tandem. You don't have to break away from old muscle memory."

"Okay. That would be fun to try sometime."

"How about now? I have a few minutes," I said, really wanting to say, "I have the rest of my life for you."

I taught her a few beach lifts and sometimes my knees were quaking a bit. What was happening to me? Twenty minutes after we first spoke we were surfing, and I was putting her in an overhead lift.

Talin and I became friends, and then we became close friends, and then we became best friends. Part of me hoped that someday there could be more than just friendship, though. As we became closer and closer as friends, it became harder and harder to suggest perhaps there could be something more. "Ah, yes," Crazy Todd lamented, "the old *switch from best friend to girlfriend* quagmire. Harder to do than the roommate switch."

Nearly six months went by and Talin returned to Sweden for a short stay because her tourist visa limited the time she could spend in the U.S. Her being halfway around the world gave me the courage to ask, "Do you think that we could ever be more than just friends?"

Immediately, she answered, "NO!"

All righty then. All engines—full speed reverse!

She remained resolute. Still, after she returned to Hawaii, I invited her to come with me as I piloted a small plane over to my favorite island of Molokai. "For dinner; you know, just friends."

Talin gave me a sideways glance. "Well, okay." The island had always had a secret and sacred draw for her too. We had discovered that both of our favorite Hawaiian songs were about that island. She had been there only once a couple of months earlier, when we flew over with a journalist from a French surf magazine, and I thought that I had caught her kind of looking at me a couple of times. Now it was just two of us with no distractions. Just her, me, and my hidden agenda.

She told me that something happened on the flight halfway between Koko Head Crater and the island of Molokai. She was watching me as I was so intent on piloting the plane, and the wall that was her fear of falling for me came down. We took off as friends, but when we landed she said everything was different. I was stunned at the way she looked at me when we dined that night at the grand lodge of the Molokai Ranch. Then she requested the song "Wahine Illikea." We danced, and we kissed for the very first time.

Had I found someone who would accept me and love me for who I was? Someone who would cherish me always, come hell or high water? Someone who would love me and even put up with me? I asked Crazy Todd for his advice. "Dude," he said, "if you can find someone who can tolerate you for more than ten minutes you better marry her."

Six months later Talin called me from a dungeon at a New Jersey airport. "Bear, Immigration won't let me in. They're sending me back."

It was my busiest workweek of the year.

"What happened?"

"They asked me why I was coming back so soon and I told them to see my fiancé. They told me I only have a tourist visa. They are sending me back."

"Pick me up at Stockholm airport the day after tomorrow. I am coming to marry you."

I made a mad dash. I bought some Hawaiian *kine* wedding rings, shoes, pants, and a jacket. Then I went back to the store and bought socks. I did not own any.

Talin met me in Stockholm, and we took the train

through the frozen land up to the small city of Falun. We spent two days surfing through all the legal requirements, then went to a cathedral in the town square and prayed quietly and said our vows before God. After that, we went across the street and the local magistrate married us.

When I looked in her eyes as we said our vows, I felt that I had not just been waiting for her for the ten years since my divorce, but that I'd actually been waiting for her my whole life. I loved her and I knew that she loved me. Just before the magistrate pronounced us married, I asked him for one additional vow.

He motioned to me, so I whispered in his ear. Then he looked at Talin, who looked at him expectantly.

"Do you, Talin, promise to tandem surf with Bear for as long as you both shall live?"

She laughed. "I do."

Good, I thought. *Let's do this man-and-wife thing and get out of here.* But Talin had another idea. She leaned over and whispered to the magistrate. He smiled and looked back at me.

"Do you, Bear, promise to keep your towels off the floor?"

That was a tough bargain, but I acquiesced, knowing I had gotten the better part of that deal.

"I now pronounce you man and wife."

Since then, we have said our vows in the Benedictine monastery, and then again three years later in Hawaii just to have an excuse to have a big party to get her whole family over here.

We did not know when or even if she would get a marriage visa, but she could not come home for perhaps a year. So we traveled together. We surfed in Sweden, Thailand, Estonia, and France, and traveled to Germany, Spain, and Italy. I had to fly back and forth to Hawaii.

Finally, we learned that Talin had an appointment at the U.S. Embassy in Stockholm. It was the last but biggest obstacle for her to come back to Hawaii. Either she would be given a visa or have to wait another ten years.

"You will be home by October thirty-first," I said to her. "I promise you." I picked her up at noon four weeks later on the thirty-first at Honolulu Airport. Finally our hearts could rest. When we got back to our condo, she looked around, and I thought she was soaking up the feeling of being home. But then I saw what she was looking at, and I leaped to pick the towel up off the floor.

The next day we walked across the sand in front of our condo and dropped our tandem surfboard in the water. She lay down in front of me and we paddled out. We paddled into the first wave, and as she got up and turned, I looked in her stunning eyes for a moment and lifted her over my head. As she was in the air, I started a new tradition. Every time we tandem surf, as she is in the first lift, I ask her the same question: "Will you marry me?" So far she has always said yes, and I don't think it is just because she does not want me to toss her and do the royal flush.

Marriage is not always easy. There are even times when it seems a bit murky. In our sojourn in Europe, we tandem surfed the Mascaret. It is the tidal bore wave near Bordeaux, France, that only breaks with twelve waves a month on the extreme tides of the new and the full. We launched our tandem board into the muddy waters of a river that was at least an eighth of a mile across. We were about fifteen kilometers upstream from the ocean. Would the single wave of the tidal bore come? We floated downstream for about fifteen minutes and then heard a mighty roar. Talin saw a head-high wave rolling around a bend in the river and flying at us upstream. She screamed at me, "Paddle!" I never saw her paddle so hard, and as the wave came we caught it easily. We tandem surfed it for more than twelve kilometers. At one point I shouted over the noise, "Fake arm to arm. Turn!" She pirouetted and, staying close to me, put her hands on my shoulders. As I flexed to lift her I called out, "Jump!" I was focusing on the river in front of us, but she was looking behind us at the swirling floodwater and she said, "NO!" I took the hint and turned her back again, and we just continued to surf as she rested against my chest.

This is the way it is with the Lord too. We want to be one with Him. We want to trust Him in the unity of betrothal, and He is faithful to us and gives us opportunities to take that leap of faith with Him. But in the murky waters of this world, if we are not always ready to leap, He still stays with us, protecting us and guiding us around the twists and turns that life takes in the hopes that in time, more and more, we will learn to rest in spiritual marriage with Him.

It was the time that the power of a new wave was heard in the land and the land was called "the married land and we were called God's delight" (see Isaiah 62:4).

13

Molokai

THE ART OF WAY FINDING

It was the time of the epic summer swell. It was the time of crossing over to promises fulfilled. It was the time when the horizon came to me.

In the darkness of the predawn hours, I walked down the path from my "surf shack" on the western shore of the peaceful island of Molokai toward the sound of the surf. I slipped my twelve-foot tandem surfboard into the waters on the bright path of the moonbeam. My eyes tracked the moonbeam across the dark sea toward where the full moon moved along its sojourn. It appeared that its journey would continue until it set right into Diamond Head Crater on the island of Oahu twenty-eight miles away. When it rose again, would it find me on that distant shore?

Molokai's peaceful, secret, sacred shores and friendly

people had saved me. I had traveled there to find uncrowded surf. I bought a "surf shack" there to escape to her *aina* (land) because of the overwhelming peace she gave me. In her, I found my times of healing. I spent hours surfing perfect waves all alone. I walked the three-mile white sand beach each day, lost in meditation as I looked for puka shells. I swim-snorkeled for miles along her shores, and hiked naked along her rocky coast. I was as isolated as I could be. I was safely away from everything in my life that tried to push me. Not having to resist by pushing back allowed me to find my true sense of balance. I heard in her voice the sound of the doves and myna birds, the sound of the wind through the palm trees, and gently breaking surf in the tidal pools.

I found in Molokai the stillness that I needed to hear God's voice again. But this was different now. I was content in His presence, not stirred up, petulant and impatiently wanting my own way. I was as a "weaned babe lying quietly against his mother's breast"(see Psalm 131:2).

As I read God's love letters to me in His word, I wrote letters back to God in my leather-bound journals. I shared with Him my thoughts, my confusion, my hurts. He heard me and I heard Him. I wrote to the giver of dreams all the new dreams that had swept into my soul. I began a new dialogue with God in a new way. I felt much more able to hear, much more able to respond. We were friends now. I had learned to want only His desires and His will, and so there came a resting in Him. I had asked Him to free my will to want His will, and He had responded. There came a trusting in His wildness that ignored my agendas, wants, and desires, and slashed and burned to set me free.

As my days of healing continued, I would find myself each late afternoon leaning against my favorite coconut tree playing my ukulele to the sound of the breeze through the palm leaves and looking out to sea toward Oahu. There came one sunset when, lost in meditation, I had dozed off and I was attacked by one of the killer coconut trees of Molokai. In civilization they trim away this heavy fruit, but in Molokai the coconuts hang heavy in the trees and one had fallen just a few inches from my head. I was thinking maybe Molokai was trying to get my attention.

And then I saw the sun, across the Kaiwi Channel, setting into Koko Head Crater on the island of Oahu. A golden orange beam of light shone across the channel right to me as if inviting me to step out and follow it like Dorothy in Oz. The thought came to me that I could paddle my tandem surfboard across that channel.

That thought had now brought me to this place, to this moment of destiny. In the predawn night, under the stars of Molokai that, in spite of the full moon, still shone brilliantly, I ventured off and paddled across the open ocean against raging current and tides to find my way to a new way of being. I would attempt to paddle across one of the gnarliest channels in the world.

I felt re-created and refreshed, ready to begin a new season in my life and to surf new swells. In me, there abided a deep assurance that I could trust the one that I had opened to in my youth and who had brought me through many heavy seas. He was the one I would trust to always have my back if I ever found myself alone in a dark alley. He had proved His faithfulness to me in spite of my own unfaithfulness again and again. It was time to cross over to live a new way.

Ancient Hawaiian *meles* (songs danced out in hula) talk story of the ancient outrigger canoe fleets that had been lost in this channel. My friend Clyde Aikau's brother and legendary waterman Eddie had died paddling near here in 1978. He had leaped from the bow of the second voyage of the double-hulled canoe the *Hokule'a*, as it began to break apart in heavy conditions of the channel.

It had nearly crossed this channel as it began a voyage to Tahiti 2,500 miles to the south. They would navigate only by using the ancient art of Polynesian "way finding" with their ability to read the stars, the ocean currents, cloud formations, and even the flight of birds to guide them. Fifteen hundred years ago, they voyaged away across thousands of miles of open sea and, more important, returned. While everyone in the "civilized" world was still hugging coastlines, Polynesians were venturing to the farther reaches of the biggest ocean. In ancient days the Tahitian kings would sometimes bless a *heau* ("temple") or a great voyaging canoe by sacrificing a *kanaka* ("commoner"). On that first day of that voyage of the *Hokule'a*, the sea required not a *kanaka* but an *ali'i*, a great "chief." And it asked for the life of the chief lifeguard of the north shore of Oahu. When the ship began to break up, Eddie Aikau threw himself on his surfboard to attempt to paddle for help. He was never seen again. But Eddie did show us the true way that day, for he laid down his life for his friends.

As I looked out to this treacherous sea, my thoughts naturally turned to Eddie's sacrifice and the *Hokule'a*. Her name means "star of gladness," reminding me that my savior is called the "bright and morning star." Her name refers to Arcturus, the zenith star for the islands of Hawaii. A voyager sailing north or south watches for this star until one night the star Hokule'a is directly overhead. This marks the latitude of the Hawaiian Islands. Then, by sailing east or west along that course, the voyager hopes to way find Hawaii.

I gazed up at the brightness of the predawn stars and I remembered my own Hokule'a, my own zenith star, the comet Hale-Bopp, as I had sojourned beneath her night after night during the dark night of my soul. She showed me the way of hope in the dark night. Now it was time for my soul to voyage, to consummate all that God had so carefully wrought in my life.

I confirmed the heading on my compass that I had set around noon the day before when I taped it to the nose of my board. I looked toward the horizon in the direction it was aiming, and saw that it was pointing directly at the moon. All I had to do was follow that moonbeam until the moon set. I would not even need to check my compass until sunrise.

I had chosen to start my paddle at this particular time on this particular day with the hope that the extreme tide of the full moon would help me as I pushed on through one of the most dangerous ocean passages in the world. On that same day, a kayaker out on a casual morning paddle along the coast just a few miles away from where I now stood, would wander just a mile offshore and get swept up in the current. By God's grace alone he was found barely alive more than two hundred miles away a few days later beyond the island of Kauai.

Watermen from around the world consider this channel the greatest of all paddling challenges. They cross it on big eight-man outrigger canoes, rotating paddlers as they leap on and off their escort boats. Others paddle on superlight carbon fiber single-man canoes and paddle hollow custom boards that are designed just for this crossing and weigh less than ten pounds. Their design allows them to catch open ocean waves and surf them for hundreds of yards, speeding them along and giving them brief respites. I estimated that with the board I chose, it could take me over twice as long.

No one who I had talked to had ever heard of anyone attempting to do what I was about to try. But I could no less leave behind my trusted surfboard for this sacred passage than a warrior could ride into battle without his trusted warhorse. Being on my tandem board was part of the sacredness of my paddle, for I was thanking tandem surfing for changing, redirecting, and enriching my life. Though the weight and design of my trusted board would add greatly to my challenge, it would also enhance my reward if I succeeded.

Just as in life, there are so many factors that throw challenges at those who venture to cross the channel. Powerful open-ocean river currents flow at different speeds at different depths of the thermal layers in the abyss of the ocean. The nearest landmass to Hawaii is more than twenty-five hundred miles away, and the currents flow uninterrupted in the two-mile-deep water only to be suddenly constricted here as the channel narrows and shallows between the two islands. The shallowing ocean depth constricts the flow as it goes from a two-mile depth in the open ocean to less than a half mile deep in the channel. The pressures of these two constrictions on the current in the channel result in a Bernoulli Effect, causing the current to speed up as it tumbles and twists its way like class-five rapids, on a massive scale, running through a narrowing canyon.

Because of the strong currents, I could not paddle directly to my safe harbor. I would have to paddle at an angle upstream to the current. The actual water distance that I would paddle was more like thirty-five miles. I knew I usually paddled about four to five miles an hour so, under average conditions, it should take me about eight hours. I wanted to schedule my departure to take complete advantage of the full moon's extreme tidal cycle.

I thought my best chance would be to paddle out when the high tide pushed me back to Molokai so that when I got close to Oahu the high tide, which would be on the rise again, would push me toward its shores when I was the most exhausted. But the conditions were not normal. My passage would take me a total of ten hours and nineteen minutes. This resulted in my having to fight the high tide at both my departure and at my arrival. I had just happened to choose to paddle on a day when an epic southern-hemi ground swell emanating from thousands miles away was beginning to push through.

The waves pushed at an odd angle to me and, as expected, they did help me for the first twenty miles. As I neared Oahu, though, I was hit by a powerful rip current. The swell grew to nearly twenty-foot faces, hitting the distant sea cliffs and cascading water nearly a hundred feet in the air and then swept back out to sea in a powerful rip. What the ground swell helped me with on the first part of the paddle it more than took back in the end when the reservoir of my strength was nearly empty.

The trade winds would begin to gently breathe as the first light of dawn shone, but soon after, they would howl at me and buffet me. The winds also Bernoullied through the island's mountains, and the change in ocean temperatures caused by the water's own Bernoulli Effect would serve to accelerate the winds as well. The winds not only blew on me, pushing my body sideways, but they blew up a surface swell and wind chop that pushed me off course. The wind swell ran at an angle to the ground swell, causing the ground swell to trip up a bit as if it were hitting a shoreline.

Many think that my greatest concern would be sharks, for they tended to feed in darkness along the reef edge at the very time I was heading out. I had seen plenty of them in Molokai as I spearfished. That was why I always "made friends" with them by trailing my catch on a longline attached to a lifeguard floatation torpedo thirty feet away from me. To me, reef sharks are mostly like dogs, and dogs are usually friendly. They would easily make me out in the light of the full moon and realize that my twelve-foot board and I were way down on their choice of menu items. However, the deeper ocean was the haunt of huge tiger and even great white sharks. It made my toes curl just to think about it.

I had duct-taped a half-size red life preserver cushion to the front of the board so I could rest my chin on it while

I paddled and I could see the compass just in front of the cushion. My friend Jeff Owens was there to see me off and called me an idiot as I left. We were always in a joking mood, but as I glanced back over my shoulder, I saw a look of trepidation on his face.

I planned on resting a total of six minutes, for I had six Gatorade bottles and I could gulp one down in less than a minute. Every minute I rested would require me to paddle three minutes to work back up against the current, so I wanted to keep my respites to a minimum.

The negative ions in the water and in the air charged my inner batteries and the feeling was magical. In the distance, across the open ocean, I could see the lights of houses and sometimes car headlights high up on the distant volcanic slopes of the island of Oahu that barely peeked above the horizon. Though the air is very clear in Hawaii, the distant island is not usually visible. The trained eye might just be able to pick it up by first looking for the unique cloud formations that bump up on the windward side as the day progresses, and then by scanning beneath them to look for just a vague outline of the island low on the horizon.

But this day was crystal clear. I almost felt like I could reach out and touch Oahu. But just like that awesome and beautiful whale that I had reached toward and tried to touch, Oahu seemed to move imperceptibly away too.

In this same way we live in a spiritual world, vaguely aware at times of the spiritual reality all around us. We all have this sense that God is watching us and hopefully watching over us. But He seems just beyond our reach. Still, there are those very real moments in life when we get a glimpse of the beatific vision, a glimpse of what it will be like to see God face-to-face, when we see in His eyes that He truly sees us and in that vision find our worth. So we try to hold on to those moments of clarity through our days, and we continue to see the unseen and reach for that which is just out of reach.

I cupped my hands, dipped them in the water, and then poured it over my head as I made the sign of the cross. "In the name of the Father, and the Son, and the Holy Spirit, I offer this passage to You, Lord." I dipped my hands in the water again, this time pouring out the water on my board, sanctifying it. I dipped my hands once more and poured the water out on the ocean as if to pour out a libation of my soul to God. I rededicated myself. "I reject all that rejects You, God. I die to myself, Lord, that You may fill me; fully infuse me with Your life that I may live only by Your will; by Your love; by Your power; by Your life."

I gave my board a push as I jumped on it. I took three deep, powerful strokes with both arms at the same time as a shout-out to the three-in-one, and then began to stroke with alternate arms. I was happy, contented, and already fulfilled just to have the chance to attempt this. The first hundred yards were easy, but then I labored a bit for the next several hundred yards. I knew that soon my blood would start flowing stronger as my lungs breathed in more deeply, filling every capillary with oxygen. Soon every muscle came to life, and I felt a surge of power.

I felt alive and exuberant. I loved this channel. I had surfed the A-frame peak called "Boilers" on her west side usually by myself, and often enough in perfect conditions, and as the day ended I would always make my way down to the shore to watch the sun set toward Oahu. The channel had become sacred to me. But how do you embrace a sunset? How do you embrace a panoramic view that is as beautiful as any woman could ever be? How do you embrace God?

With this crossing, I would caress every inch of this body of water and in so doing I would make her mine and she would make me hers. The abyss of this channel was my sacramental of the very depth of God. I rolled my shoulders to paddle deep into her crystal clear waters and continued to paddle for nearly an hour as I glanced sideways to check my bearings from time to time.

I had done a lot of distance paddling along shorelines. In preparation for this paddle, I had recently paddled about half the distance I was about to attempt when I went from the Arch at Anacapa Island to the surf spot called "the Strand" at Channel Islands harbor near Ventura, California. It was considered an epic paddle by most watermen. It was something no one had ever heard of being done before.

But today's paddle would be twice as far and the conditions exponentially more daunting. But still, it was just one mile, one paddle stroke at a time. As my sensei Bill Poett once said when beads of sweat pooled beneath me as I did push-ups, "Anyone can do just one more of anything."

Polynesians would way find by looking back. They would set a signal fire high on a mountain and then farther up and behind it they would set another signal fire. If the way-finders sailed on a course that lined those two points up, they would eventually see similar signal fires on the island beyond the horizon. So it is that I began my paddle by look-ing back over my life.

As I pushed off, I felt that same awakening, that same going forth of my spirit before me, as on that day long ago on the beach when, as a boy-almost-man, I first perceived that God was eternal, infinite, and all powerful. Wonder overtook the boy in me and had made me a man. Wonder had made me stand up. My gaze became fixed on this dis-tant awesome God. How could anything be the same after that? In the ocean I had seen the Holy Grail. In her I saw the abyss of God's love. But just as in the myth of the Holy Grail, it was taken from me. And so my life's desire became to drink from the Holy Grail of the ocean and of God's love that it drew me to. To go deep in the wave of God.

I was in awe of God and even afraid of Him. I was well aware of my own unworthiness and the need for purging and purification. My focus was obedience more than relationship. My spiritual focus was not found in prayer but more in that I *ought to* pray. I did not find spiritual solace in reading the word. I read the word because I *ought to*. I did not know then that prayer and meditating on His word was like an Indiana Jones secret passageway to the very adventurous experience of the presence of God. My infant spirituality was caught up in the *ought to* feelings: I *ought to* do this; I *ought not do* that.

My spirituality consisted of trying on my own strength to live up to God's standards, to strive to be up*right*, which really only made me up*tight* because I could never quite live up to my own expectations. I was doing it all on my own strength and seeking more to appease God than to please Him. I had not learned yet that righteousness came by trusting in Him who alone is righteous. But I was making my first steps toward intimacy, and one day I would experience "righteousness and peace kiss" (Psalms 85:10 NIV).

I paddled hard now against the current of the high tide that pulled me back toward land. Even so, in the awakening of my youth I turned away from the pull of the world system of its excitements and enticements. Just as a surfer gazes out to sea with his back to the world, so I became fixated on more eternal things and the pull of the world, though always present, had limited effect on me. When wrestling as a child, if someone grabbed me from behind, I just ignored him. As he held on to my jacket, I just slipped out of it, leaving it in his hands. What drew so many of my peers held nothing on me. I just slipped away. I had begun to learn the lessons of detachment. Even now, as I had to paddle hard to pull away from the tide that was pulling me back, all I felt was hope and all I focused on was the now of the next paddle stroke.

Finally, after about an hour, I paddled beyond sacred La'au Point and I felt the tidal current release me, and the first push of the building ground swell. That is how it is. The safety of the safe harbor only holds us back, but once we break out to the open sea to pursue the true desires that only God can place in our heart of hearts, we break free from that limiting pull of the safety of sameness. The safety of routine and comfort keeps us from abandoning all and venturing in pursuit of the wildness of God's high calling to intimacy with Him. Hawaiian tradition says that the spirits of those who have died depart from La'au Point to cross over to a new dimension of life. I felt my spirit rise up too, as if to depart into a new dimension in my life.

Paddling provides me with the same Zen of the here and now of meditation that walking and pedaling do. I began to feel myself slip into that still point. As I paddle or pedal or walk, I find myself quieting the linear thought processes of worries, cares, agendas, and ambitions to drift into the now of the eternal presence of God. God's very name, Yahweh, means "I am who am." He lives in the eternal now. His son reinforced this when He said, "Before Abraham was 'I am.'" His son's name, Yeshua, translates to Joshua or Jesus and means "I am who am Salvation." In other words, the now of this moment is always the moment to open to Him. I began to breathe out the name of Jesus and meditate on the work He had done in me, in spite of me. How sweet to be suspended a mile above the depth of the sea. I began to slide into the sweetest meditation of the abyss, the very depth of God.

I sensed the sky barely change hue as the sun, still far below the horizon at my back, began to announce its ascension and I awaited that first puff that would announce the coming of the trade winds. As I paddled, I kept my senses alert to breathe in that first breath of dawn. Then it was as if God himself had awakened and I felt the very *ha* of God as a single puff of wind blew over me. The darkness of the water below me began to show a deep blue, while above me the stars began to blink out. In the latitudes, near the equator, the sun rises and sets rapidly, and so it was that within twenty minutes of first light the sun burst above the horizon at my back and I felt its warmth even as the rising trade winds cooled me. I looked back and saw the sun shining at the same level on the horizon as the full and very bright moon. *They are smiling at each other*, I thought, and so I smiled at God for I knew that I was meant to reflect His light.

I knew that the moon is only moon dust and can only shine as the sun shines on it and I recalled how I had sensed in my youth my own worthlessness. That I was just darkness and emptiness unless God found value in me. And that day when I was in college at the house of the rocket scientist, His light had exploded on me and in me and I became as the moon infused with the brightness of His truth and His love.

I had heard that God was love, but my feelings said something different. Guilt hung around my neck like seaweed and I constantly judged myself trying hard, not knowing that I was to rest in God and He would transform me. I sensed that He was judging me and not happy with me and it robbed me of any joy. When they prayed for me that night in Texas, all that changed as the bright and morning star, the son of God, rose within me and in one moment shined on me and infused me not just with His love and His light and His forgiveness but with a knowing. I knew Him who was beyond all knowing! It was only a glimpse, but in that moment of the infusion of His Spirit, I knew His heart and I knew His thoughts.

I continued to paddle, and as the sun began to rise behind me, the brilliant golden light seemed to empower me even more. With the brightness of dawn and the new push of the ground swell behind me and to my left, the paddling seemed to get almost effortless as I flew across the channel. Most of the conditions were in my favor. I tried not to look back, but when I did, I saw Molokai fading behind me rapidly. This was going to be easy. This took no faith at all. I was flying across the channel. Only four hours had gone by and already Oahu seemed closer than Molokai.

It reminded me of that honeymoon period after the great tsunami of God's love had swept through me and swept me up. I had thought, *This is perfect. I have arrived. I am riding the perfect wave and I am feeling pretty damn close to perfect myself.* I thought that I had arrived. I had God on my terms and life was easy.

Molokai was fading behind me and so I made two new lineup points on Oahu. As I checked them, it was becoming obvious that the lateral current was growing stronger and I needed to angle more and more steeply to my right. I kept my paddle speed the same, but as I did I could feel my muscles tightening up a bit. Maybe this wasn't going to be as easy as I thought. And I recalled how the same thing had happened to me early on after my experience of the infusion of God's love. I prayed, "Lord, I love You with all my heart. All I am is Yours." But then I heard the Holy Spirit whisper, "Really?" And He pointed to the core of my being and just simply asked again "Really?" as He pointed to my desire to fall madly in love and to raise a family.

My response was a feeble, "Uhhh, how about this? You can have everything but that." Fail! I doubted that God's will could be as cool as mine. It was a foolish thought. I came to learn that even though I am not faithful, God is always faithful and He did His work in me and worked into me the *want* to want to. I had surrendered this biggest thing to Him and that made it easier to learn to surrender the smaller things and to seek to live my life in docility to the adventure of His perfect will. I began to learn to surf His waves.

As I paddled on, I set my chin on the soft floatation cushion and stared at the bearing of my compass and adjusted more and more to head up current as the lateral drift became stronger. As the going got tough, I recalled the season in my life when my responsibilities weighed down on me, and His words *Take up your cross daily and follow me* became my anthem. The feelings of adventure that came with the feeling of intimacy with God had been choked out by the worries of providing for my family, and I was spiritually dry. My soul was parched and arid with no sense of God's grace.

Now here I was in the midst of the deep ocean, with no joy and maybe even a little fear. All I could do was just keep my chin down and keep going, and it felt the same as that season in my life when my personal time with God became nonexistent until finally, when I was near the breaking point, God had whispered to me "You are My walking man. Come walk with Me a ways." I had begun my walk and talk with God and that laid the pattern in my life of walking, pedaling, and now paddling into the Zen of prayer and the experience of His presence. And in that time, God surprised me and returned me to the ocean and to surfing.

The sun was directly overhead now, shining deep into the translucent, radiant blue of the sea. Though it was not easy, I was still up to the challenge. Everything seemed to still be going my way. I forgot for long minutes that I was even out paddling. I remembered the season in my life that was like this. I was married, had four children, a house in the nicest neighborhood, and even a mountain cabin. Though my health waned with the growing back pain, my business flourished.

I was lost in reverie when my thoughts were suddenly disrupted. A huge shadow had just passed beneath my board. Was it a manta ray? Yes, yes, that's what it was. There it was again. Hmm. Manta rays don't circle like that, but sharks do. I knew it was not a reef shark. It had to be a tiger or, worse, a great white. I kept my paddle speed constant but tried to gracefully dip my hands in and pull them out cleanly. I did not want to make any sort of thrashing like a wounded or scared animal might make.

More than a half hour passed without it circling back. I began to relax enough to fall into my reverie again, and I recalled that season in my life when God in His wildness was on the attack as He circled me and hunted me. He had whispered to me, "Everything that can be shaken will be shaken and everything that can be taken will be taken."

God became like a tiger shark on the hunt as He hunted down every false attachment that I had that was not of Him. I came to know what He meant in His love letter when He called Himself "a jealous God" (see Exodus 20:5).

I continued to paddle for another hour. The currents were so strong that I was miles away still and yet already past the time when I thought I would arrive. Then something very strange happened and a sensation came over me that I had never felt before. It felt like my body was breaking down. I felt something like strings along my forearms and legs and then soon afterward a tingling, then a stinging, and then finally a consuming burning. Was I falling apart? Were my very capillaries breaking down under the challenge? Soon I was racked with pain.

I knelt on my board to catch my mental and emotional breath and when I did so I saw how far I really was from either shore. But as I scanned the horizon I saw that I had been paddling through what looked like acres of man-o'-war jellyfish who'd been stinging me with their long tentacles. At least I knew what was going on, but I feared the symptoms would increase to paralyzing pain and perhaps even result in my muscles locking up.

I recalled seeing a paraglider once land in the middle of a huge cactus patch and he knew as I knew now that his only way out was to just go through it. I had no choice. I had to keep paddling through them. I prayed for God to protect me and I prayed that even as He had healed my back that He would heal me now. I remembered how I had learned that "when I am weak it is then that I am strong" (see 2 Corinthians 12:10), for then it is by God's power and might that I was healed and lived again without pain. My back healing was unwarranted and undeserved but it pleased God and He healed me.

My blood must have been flowing so strong and clean that within forty-five minutes the pain had relented and was only a tingling again. I was so close now and I had to resist the urge to sprint to the finish. I thought I could be there in forty-five minutes or so. But then I felt the conditions around me rapidly deteriorate. The ground swells had been building throughout the day, but that did not help me much because I could not catch them on my heavy tandem board. Now, in the distance, I could see them exploding against the cliffs and I felt something I never expected. I felt the powerful rip river flowing right back at me off Oahu, which lay at least four miles away.

It was relentless, but I paddled on, though I felt for the first time I might be fighting a losing battle. I had expected the help of the high tide pushing me in but I was arriving late, and now added to this riptide was a receding tidal current pulling me away from Oahu. I dared not stop to drink. I could not risk resting and losing any of my hard-earned progress. I had aimed east toward Makapu'u, but the lateral current kept pushing me west, and I now I was drifting sideways two miles past Sandy Beach.

I had no choice but to lower my head and angle even more directly into the current and wind chop. I feared that it would push me west right past Oahu and back out to sea. The seas grew turbulent, and I was being bounced around as I tried to keep my course true. An hour went by, and I could tell I had gotten just a bit closer now, but I had drifted another two miles west to Hanauma Bay. I turned my board more and more upwind, trying to fight the current. I paddled with all my might and prayed, "God, I need You. Give me Your strength."

It felt again like I was pedaling into the teeth of Tropical Storm Allison. When I had to pedal hard just to go down a mountain and I had seen the grudge that I had held toward God and forgave Him, I learned there would always be mountains, there would always be giants in the land, and there would always be mountain waves, but through them He would reveal to me His awesome greatness and impart His *manna* to me.

I drifted past Hanauma Bay and now saw Hawaii Kai and the harbor buoy that marked my planned narrow entrance to the safety of shore. I kept making limited headway but soon I was drifting past the harbor buoy. I had no choice now but to turn my board directly upstream as I drifted by the harbor. With Black Point, the final point of land, in the distance. I knew if I did not get in there, I would be blown right past and out to sea again. Because the surf was breaking so big, there was only one narrow window to make it into the harbor and that was through the deep narrow boat channel marked by a buoy.

I looked down and prayed, "Not by might, not by power, by your Spirit, Lord." I paddled, staring at the buoy, willing it to come to me. I sprint paddled for forty-five minutes, battling for every inch that I gained. But I could tell I was getting closer. For every minute of the hardest paddling yet, I gained only one hundred feet. I was in the harbor now, but the winds were even stronger, vortexing through the mountains. The gusts pouring through this wind tunnel pushed me sideways away from my goal, but the rip current had finally started to lessen and the buoy was less than a mile away now. And then less than half a mile.

I could see great waves from the southern hemi swell launching over it. That's just not supposed to happen to a harbor buoy. Thirty more minutes and I would be there if I could just keep paddling. Then suddenly I was at the buoy. It was surging and bouncing as the waves exploded around it, but I grabbed on to it and clung to it and sat up on my board only to have a giant wave crush me against it so hard that I thought it would rip off my leg at the knee. But

I had made it to the narrow gap, the only way to safety, and I remembered how I had learned the simple singularity that Jesus was The Way.

I looked back and saw a fifteen-foot wave opening its jaws to consume me. I turned toward shore and paddled harder than I had all day and dropped into the face of God's wave. I rocketed forward in the impact zone, clinging to the rails of my board because I had no leash. I just went with the power of the wave, making no effort except to rest in it and stay in the center of its power. It seemed that the land a half mile away came flying toward me. It was as if with that wave God had been the first to greet me and He had said, "Well done, my son," and given me a push like the exhilarating push that my dad used to give me when I was learning to ride a bike.

I was one with the wave. The way to perfection is simple; it is just an active yielding to the wildness of His will and in this way to be one with Him as I had learned tandem surfing and shooting that narrow gap during the first world title. It was at-one-ment with His will.

Then I was there. No more motion in the ocean. I was in the peaceful, quiet, still waters only an eighth of a mile from shore. I saw in the distance my *ohana*, my family. They were there to greet me as I arrived. I had asked them to bring carbs, protein, and lots of water.

They had laid out a picnic blanket, and as we sat there

feasting, I thought of how God had taught me that I was to be His betrothed and that His ultimate goal for my intimacy with Him was a marital type of love. I looked at the peanut butter and jelly sandwiches and thought that this was not exactly the wedding feast of the lamb. But it felt like it.

God has a secret place of quietness and peace in each of us. Within each of us we have the island of Molokai. You have to push and paddle toward the horizon and if you do the horizon will come to you.

Surf, my friends. Go deep in the wave and God will make Himself known to you. Gaze on Him who gazes at you. Love and know Him who loves and knows you and who wants to reveal Himself to you. The only way we can see Him, though, is to let Him take us on a journey of transformation of becoming more like Him. "For we shall be like Him, for we shall see Him as he really is" (see John 3:2). There is no depth of intimacy with Him unless you go to hell and back just like His son did. For He has promised, "If you seek me I will let you find me. If you seek me with all your heart I will let you find me" (see Jeremiah 29:12–13). He invites us to abandon ourselves to the wildness of His will and love, which is His very presence.

You like go deep?

About the Author

BEAR WOZNICK was born September 21, 1953, in Powers Lake, North Dakota. He is a two-time world champion tandem surfer and cofounder and ambassador of the International Tandem Surfing Association for serious competitors, as well as founder of The BearsWave.com Tandem Expression Teams for those who simply want to enjoy the beauty and art of tandem. He is featured in Fuel TV's *Clean Break* series, is the subject of the film project *The Bear—Going Deep*, and hosts weekly podcasts on BearsWave.com. Bear has surfed on four continents and even more oceans. He is acknowledged as having revived the ancient art of tandem surfing and he won the Duke OceanFest Masters World Tandem Surfing Title in 2007 and 2008.

Bear has twice run with the bulls in Pamplona, once on the bloodiest day in its history. He is a licensed pilot and he skydives. He holds the very rare ninja black belt. Bear is also licensed in scuba and enjoys being a well-rounded waterman—sailing, spearfishing, distance paddling, and surfing his outrigger canoe. He paddled his surfboard out to the dangerous waves of Teahopu'u in Tahiti on a huge forty-foot day that came to be known as Bloody Sunday, the bloodiest day in the history of surfing. Bear paddled his surfboard across thirty-five miles of treacherous open ocean between Moloka'i and O'ahu. He has pedaled his bicycle across the United States from San Diego, California, to Jacksonville, Florida.

Bear lives with his wife, national gymnastics champion and chef Talin Heurlin, on the beach in Waikiki, Hawaii, where he has his own firm as a CPA.

Bear is proud parent to Fawn, Jeremiah, Shane, and Joshua.

Visit Bear's website, BearsWave.com, and Facebook page, BearsWave.com, reach him on Twitter @BearsWave, and listen to his weekly BearsWave.com podcast on iTunes or YouTube.